Daily Reflections II
Bible-based Lyrical Verse

JOHN ALEXANDER

DEDICATION

This book of poems is dedicated to my wife who first encouraged me to share them, to those who read them and encouraged me to continue, and to those who may be encouraged by them.

CONTENTS

ACKNOWLEDGMENTS

This book is a compilation of poems written during my quiet time shared to provide you the reader an opportunity to read a lyrical poem from my heart to yours each day of the year.

I wish to acknowledge my wife for her patience and encouragement as I write and for her seeds of inspiration to get me started.

I want to thank the Mockingbird chapter of the Poetry Society of Texas for the feedback and encouragement to continue writing.

A special offer of thanks and gratitude goes out to friends in the Marathon Class and the Men's Bible study group at Stonebriar Community Church for their interest and encouragement as I continue to write.

A thank you goes out to my daughter Christina for her feedback as I write. Her input as a former literary arts teacher means a lot to me.

I extend a thank you to friends and followers on Facebook who are a constant stream of encouragement as they read my initial words.

I extend a thank you to friends who read and comment as I continue to write poems most days and share them online at www.QuietTimeRhymes.com

JANUARY 1, A GIFT

The ripe old age of seven five,
I'm grateful still to be alive.
It seems that with each passing year,
I cherish days and hold them dear.

When I was asked to leave, retire,
I found new ways I could inspire,
Wrote books for children, fun to read,
And in their hearts to plant a seed.

God prompted me in quiet time
To share my heart with words of rhyme.
My wife then urged me, "Set them free.
Don't hide the words, let others see."

This cherished gift I share with you,
"Reach out to God. His love is true."

JANUARY 2, JOY AND PEACE

No matter what the year may bring
May you find joy, may your heart sing.
May you find peace in spite of storms,
God's love inside to keep you warm.

Life brings the best and worst of times.
Our roots reach deep through dirt and grime
To gain the strength we need to grow.
Look up and feel God's love and know

Our life on earth is not the end.
No matter what's around the bend
God's love's eternal, pure, and strong.
He walks with us the whole day long.

May you know joy and peace this year
Throughout the ups and downs and tears.

JANUARY 3, A NEW YEAR

If you're reading these lines you've begun a new year,
Giving thanks for the days in the past you've been through,
For the loved ones you cherish, the friends you hold dear,
But also embracing a future that's new.

It's a time to look forward, to start a new page,
As we make resolutions, I pray they include
Finding ways to connect, to converse and engage,
To see a real face, not just clips we have viewed.

Let's savor the moments the times that we share.
It's not really hard to reach out, be a friend.
I've seen others show kindness I know it's not rare.
Finding ways to connect helps us all in the end.

I pray that the kindness and love that we show
Will touch those around us and blossom and grow.

JANUARY 4, A SERVANT'S HEART

Surround me Lord with humble folk
Who serve because they've learned from You,
Who take to heart the words You spoke,
Who've come to know those words are true.

Regardless of the task at hand,
What role or service they perform,
They gladly do and understand
A servant's heart is not the norm.

So many hearts are filled with pride.
Accomplishment, achieving goals
Can lead to arrogance inside.
A cancer forms within the soul.

Lord help me humbly do my part.
Instill in me a servant's heart.

JANUARY 5, THE LORD'S STRENGTH

There's nothing like faith in the Lord up above
To give me the courage I need every day.
One who gave up His life so that I could know love
Is the leader I follow, He shows me the way.

He provides me the confidence, not in myself,
But in One with authority. He's in control.
His Words are not something to keep on a shelf
But rather to read and absorb in my soul.

The Lord keeps me stable and steadfast and strong.
I'm grateful for blessings preserved in His Word.
Lord keep me from evil, the things that are wrong.
Lord lift my heart daily to soar like a bird.

Lord You give me strength and the courage to stand.
You hold my life in the palm on Your hand.

JANUARY 6, WORDS TO SERVE

Instill in me the will to serve
With proper motives simple, pure,
My words and actions when observed
Be found congruent, wise, mature.

As I pen words to fill each page
To share in rhyme what's in my heart,
I pray my words improve with age,
More love, compassion to impart.

I pray the words I write and share
Will help another known God's love,
Reach out to Him when life's unfair,
Find peace descending like a dove.

Lord help me always lift Your name,
In simple words Your love proclaim.

JANUARY 7, EACH LIFE

Each life's a biography etched over time,
Each day a narrative, sometimes in rhyme.
Each line is written by actions we take,
Some of them good, some we deem a mistake.

Some days bring us closure a chapter will end,
A time to reflect, let a new phase begin.
Life can't be edited, changed, or erased.
Time marches forward, it cannot be chased.

The future's not written, it's something we write.
I pray up ahead that the sunshine is bright.
Each day that I live I pray something I do
Helps someone discover their story's not through.

There's more to be written each day that we live.
The pages are gilded by love that we give.

JANUARY 8, IN HIS IMAGE

We're each one imprinted, the image of God,
Not just a creature, an empty facade.
Inside He implanted a vacuum, a space
Longing for love and His marvelous grace.

In all of creation mankind's set apart,
Body and soul mixed with love in our heart.
Confined for a time to this body on earth
Our spirit lives on we were given at birth.

Our maker, creator has formed us to love
Those who surround us and God up above,
The greatest commandment, the sum of them all.
If only we'd listen and answer His call.

One day He'll return, and we'll worship and sing,
Acknowledge our maker, creator, and King.

JANUARY 9, YOUR LIGHT

Throw open the shutters, let light in my soul.
May the creatures of darkness let loose of their hold.
May Your goodness and mercy take over my heart,
Provide me discernment, Your wisdom impart.

Let Your Word shine within me, enlighten my mind,
Provide me the insight to share what I find.
Lord give me the courage to write what I see,
Not looking at others but starting with me.

Lord clean out the clutter that blocks out the light,
Help me let in the sunshine, it's no longer night.
Lord drive out the darkness and fill me with song,
A song of Your love that makes right every wrong.

Help me write verses that take flight and soar,
Enriched and enlightened, share words that restore.

JANUARY 10, FOOLISH NOTIONS

What foolish notions spring from pride.
They wall us off, we're trapped inside,
Afraid to share, let others see.
End selfish pride, Lord set us free.

Pretensions form an empty shell
And keep us locked inside a cell,
Believe a lie, remain aloof.
Whatever happened to the truth?

Deception cloaks a soul in pain
Repeating empty words in vain.
It's time to speak the truth aloud,
Call out the lies, ignore the proud.

Lord help us see Your truth, Your light.
Help us discern the wrong from right.

JANUARY 11, TRIALS AND FAITH

At times when our life seems about to derail
We find out if our faith can stay strong and endure,
Though we know that the Lord in the end will prevail.
When tested our faith can grow strong and mature.

In all shapes and sizes the large and the small
The troubles and trials are all part of life.
No one avoids them they come to us all.
No one's immune to the troubles and strife.

Walk with the Lord in the beauty of spring.
See the beauty of roses, each petal, each leaf.
Let the Lord fill our heart, so we learn how to sing.
May our faith remain strong through life's sorrow and grief.

I pray through each struggle our faith can grow strong.
May God bless us with joy, may our heart fill with song.

JANUARY 12, BREATHE EASY

I've come to embrace a more simplified day,
One that brings no surprises, no good news or bad.
Time alone before dawn helps me view it that way,
Allowing my soul to breathe easy, be glad

That the Lord has allowed me these silver edged years,
A time to slow down and a time to reflect
On the past that's been marked by both gladness and tears,
To spend time with the people I love and respect.

I don't know years that the future may hold,
But I now know the number is not my concern.
I trust in the Lord, He's the one in control,
No matter what lies up ahead 'round the turn.

I pray that no matter what future days bring,
My heart still rejoices, continues to sing.

JANUARY 13, LOVE AND GRACE

It's not yet light. The house is still.
Lord guide my hand. Let Your words spill
Upon the page. Lord help me write
With verses pleasing in Your sight.

Help me convey, with words that flow,
Your love inside, Lord let it grow.
Invade my heart, my soul, my mind,
Swing wide the door, love's not confined.

Lord walk with me along life's trail.
Lord let Your love in me prevail.
I pray You guide my thoughts today,
The words I write, the words I say.

May others find their resting place
Wrapped in Your arms of love and grace.

JANUARY 14, A BLANK PAGE

A blank page before me that's yet to be filled,
The words not yet written, the lines are not done.
I could write about weather, the dawn and the chill,
Or just jot down my thoughts, let them flow and have fun.

But I'll try to dig deeper and share from my heart,
Try to find words that come up from my soul.
Perhaps there's some wisdom I'll find to impart,
Or instead I'll determine that's not the main goal.

The Bible is filled with the wisdom we need.
Who am I to embellish with words of my own?
Today I encourage you, take time to read.
God's in control, He still sits on the throne.

Lord grant us the wisdom we need for today.
May we focus on You as we fill up each page.
Help us discern what You have to convey,
As we walk with You daily through every life stage.

JANUARY 15, ARROGANCE

I shy away from ones who boast,
The arrogance I dislike most.
The selfishness that grows with pride
Can etch away the good inside.

I much prefer humility
In those with great ability,
Who honor God and lift Him up,
Seek after Him to fill their cup.

God's gifts and talents from above
Should graciously be shared in love.
Develop them, refine a skill,
Then seek the Lord, His path, His will.

Just serve the Lord, give Him your best,
And know each day you're truly blessed.

JANUARY 16, CHOOSE JOY

As I search for the words to describe how I feel,
And reach deep in my heart to share something that's real,
I pray I'm reflecting God's light from above,
The words that I share are expressions of love.

At times when I'm weary and troubles abound
I need time with the Lord, morning silence, no sound.
That time, early morning, to read and to pray
To help me refocus, prepare for the day,

Remember the Lord is in charge of my life.
His Spirit's inside me through troubles and strife.
Why should I choose worry, get all weighted down,
When the Lord offers joy and a smile not a frown?

Lord You are the love that I find in my heart.
You bring joy every morning before the day starts.

JANUARY 17, FRAGILE

Life can be fragile, like paper, so thin.
Consider it precious, a gift from the Lord.
Each morning I'm grateful a new day begins.
Lord help me live wisely not worried or bored.

Lord You hold the future, my life's in Your hand.
You give me breath, every beat of my heart.
Lord help me find wisdom, to see, understand.
May I share love with others before I depart.

Lord guide me, direct me, and show me the way,
The pathway each day that I spend on this earth.
Lord help me live life to the fullest each day.
I pray that my actions each day will have worth.

Lord open my heart so I clearly can see.
Help me focus on others, life's not about me.

JANUARY 18, HOLD LOOSELY

It's hard to let go of the ones we hold dear.
It's easy to grip them with all of our might.
If we hold them more loosely, not grip them in fear,
We'll find joy, not regret as we see them take flight.

Whether parent or child or a friend that we know,
If we do for another the things they could do,
We can overprotect and not help them to grow,
Not help them to learn how to try something new.

Although it is difficult loosening our grip,
But it's better than choosing to not love at all.
Although we may struggle, occasionally trip,
The Lord picks up when we stumble and fall.

Lord help us know balance, not helping too much,
Not creating dependence on us as a crutch.

JANUARY 19, LEARNING TO SERVE

More focus on others and less on my needs,
Always remembering others in prayer,
Helps me learn how to serve, how to follow God's lead.
Lord I need Your help daily to love and to care.

If my heart and my soul remains focused on You,
If I read Your word daily, continue to pray,
I'll more easily see what You'd have me to do,
More easily speak what You'd have me to say.

I pray that Your Spirit will help me discern
How I can serve, the right places to go.
Lord teach me each day, I have so much to learn,
How best to serve others, so much I don't know.

I'll continue to write, may You bless every word.
I pray as I share that Your message is heard.

JANUARY 20, GOD'S CREATURES

One day I was blessed by a symbol of love
On the fence near our holly so still and serene,
God's beauty and grace in the form of a dove
Amidst the red berries and leaves brilliant green.

When Lucy spied it, perhaps heard it coo,
She stood very still as she watched near the ledge.
She patiently watched it until the dove flew.
She seemed sad when it left, disappeared near a hedge.

I think she remembers each day near the fence,
She looks up to see if the dove will return.
Although she keeps looking, we've not seen him since.
I'm always amazed at how quickly she learns.

God's creatures amaze me the big and the small.
Each one is unique. He created them all.

JANUARY 21, GIVING

Do you find yourself living, just plodding along,
Without motivation, not eager to rise?
Be thankful each day, you can breathe and stay strong.
Don't let fear and doubt be your final demise.

Find your purpose in life and you'll learn how to live.
God made you unique and there's no one like you.
Dig deep and discover the ways you can give.
You'll find life refreshing, each day will be new.

Trust in the Lord. He will guide you each day.
Reach out and ask Him, the Lord's always near.
He'll give you direction and show you the way.
Take time to listen and let your heart hear.

I pray that I've shared an encouraging word.
It's my way of giving. I pray that it's heard.

JANUARY 22, IN GOD WE TRUST

I don't know where or when or how,
But evil's spread across our land.
Our apathy is rampant now.
Is no one left to take a stand?

When did the change in us begin,
Embracing things we know are wrong,
Despise the ones who call it sin?
I pray for those who sing God's song,

Who humbly bow their heads in prayer,
Reach out to God and seek his face,
Turn from the wicked ways we share,
Turn back to God, His love embrace.

We serve a God who's also just.
I pray it's true, "In God we trust."

JANUARY 23, A GRUDGE

I'm often quick to hold a grudge.
I find it harder to forgive.
I know it's not for me to judge,
That's not the way I want to live.

Why is it hard to see the good,
And find the words I need to say?
Lord help me see the way I should.
May bitter thoughts just fade away.

Lord you forgive, what right have I
To let an act or deed take hold?
When I forgive, I'm free to fly.
Your love and peace can fill my soul.

I pray we all can learn to soar,
Let go of hate, find peace once more.

JANUARY 24, SEEKING LIGHT

A flower blooms in springtime,
　it sprouts up through the ground.
The seedling stays in darkness
　beneath the winter cold
Searching for the sunshine,
　where only mud is found.
The longing breaks the seedling's shell,
　it's heart can then unfold.

The roots find food and nourishment,
　the tiny seedling grows.
It pushes up through stubborn sod,
　keeps reaching for the light.
It seems to me a miracle,
　a tiny seedling knows
To make its way up through the ground,
　it's only known the night.

Some seeds they never seek the light,
　they never seem to bloom.
They live instead below the ground
　where they prefer to stay.
I do not know why they would choose
　the cold, the dark, the doom.
Inside the darkness void of light,
　they soon will rot, decay.

Perhaps they need a helping hand
　to help them see the choice.
Someone to share the words of love,
　with kind and caring voice.

JANUARY 25, GOD'S REALM

Lord help me to fathom the depths of Your realm,
To understand fully what You have in store.
Lord help let go and have You at the helm.
Eternity's boundless I'd love to know more.

The treasures God's shared, although centuries old,
His people, through history have captured each word,
Preserved through the ages, recorded on scrolls.
And those who knew Jesus wrote down what they heard.

I'm grateful for Bibles, so many in print,
So easily purchased, distributed, shared.
Its books probe the depths, let us know the extent
Of God's love for His people and how much He cared.

His love is extended to you and to me,
That limitless, boundless eternity free.

JANUARY 26, WEARY DAYS

Do you long for some days when there's not much to do,
A few days to linger and just hang around,
Instead of those days thinking "Lord get me through,"
Those days filled with turmoil, life's coming unwound?

I pray you find peace in the midst of the strife.
Just whisper a prayer knowing God's in control.
Perhaps it's a loved one, a husband, or wife.
May you find the Lord's comfort down deep in your soul.

Lord at times we grow weary, the load's hard to bear.
We need Your help daily to carry the weight.
You're always beside us, we're grateful You're there.
You're the One in control, our life's not left to fate.

Our life here on earth like a vapor will fade,
But Your spirit's inside us eternally made.

JANUARY 27, SEEKING

So many are hurting and asking, "Lord why?"
Perhaps it's beyond what our minds comprehend.
God knows every tear as it falls when we cry.
The Lord provides comfort, helps broken hearts mend.

Like a child on a journey that keeps asking 'When',
How long must we wait for the answer to prayer?
Perhaps it's today, or it's just 'round the bend,
Or perhaps it's been answered, we're just not aware.

Our prayers are important but seeking God's will
Is what matters most in our journey through life.
If we trust in the Lord as we climb every hill,
We're surrounded in love as we're walking through strife.

Lord my life's in Your hands and I trust You know best.
I know You're beside me through every life test.

JANUARY 28, COURAGE TO SHARE

Some call it traditional others old fashioned,
I love my words metered and flowing with rhyme.
Now poetry's changed, even rhythm is shunned.
That seed that was planted way back in my prime

Was encased in a pod that took fire to reveal.
Once it broke open the seedling took root,
Broke through to the sunlight and learned how to feel.
When I look in the mirror and see that old coot,

I stare and I ask him, "What took you so long?
Why keep words inside you that could have been said?
Throughout your whole life did you get it all wrong?
Or was it worthwhile that you waited instead?"

Perhaps all along words were forming inside.
They took decades of life to take shape and to grow.
The words were all there they just learned how to hide.
Through the rhyme and the rhythm, they learned how to flow.

I'm still finding words that were hidden somewhere.
I help them find courage and learn how to share.

JANUARY 29, COMPASSION

I pray for compassion, the will to discern,
To listen to others and hear their concerns.
At times it's not answers, advice, even words,
But rather to listen, reflect what I've heard.

Lord give me the wisdom to know when to hush,
Respect for the silence, show patience, not rush.
To take time to listen, to hear with my heart,
Can show more compassion than words can impart.

Lord grant me the empathy I need today
To focus on hearing what others may say.
Hear not just the words, but the feelings they share.
Then help me to know how to show that I care.

I've known Your compassion. Your love I've embraced.
Help me show others Your love, and Your grace.

JANUARY 30, DISCOVERY

I love to discover, see what I can find,
On the backroads and byways, not on the main path,
And also discover what's inside my mind,
Beyond just technology, science, or math.

The year I turned seventy I fell in love,
Discovered a passion for writing in rhyme.
The words swirled around me below and above,
They each formed a rhythm one word at a time.

I love to hear words as they dance in my head,
To capture a thought from my heart in my brain.
To try to find words to express what it said,
Then write them all down as they form a refrain.

I pray they're not babble that none comprehend,
But rather give comfort when shared with a friend.

JANUARY 31, DEPTH OF LOVE

When hurts cut deep into the soul,
From deep within there comes a groan,
When desolation takes its toll,
Reach out to God. You're not alone.

The God whose Son came here to die
Can mend the lonely broken hearts.
I can't conceive the depth of why,
But know His love will not depart.

The Lord will help the hurts to mend,
Help ease the pain until it's gone.
He's always there, a constant friend.
You'll never need to walk alone.

I pray you know God's love inside.
God's love runs deep, in Him confide.

FEBRUARY 1, ALONG THE WAY

I'm well beyond that middle age.
I've made it to life's final stage,
That final quarter of my days.
I pray I'm strong this final phase.

Sometimes I like to reminisce …
The memories of ones I miss.
But I prefer to live each day
By sharing life to help some way.

We each have walked a different road,
Each carrying a different load.
We each can lend a helping hand,
Provide support, help someone stand.

Sometimes it only takes a smile,
Perhaps just visit for a while,
Or read aloud, take time to share,
It's little things that show we care.

I pray I help along the way
By things I do and words I say.

FEBRUARY 2, WINTER'S CHILL

The freezing rain, the sleet, the cold,
The icy shards, the crunching sound,
My bones I know are getting old.
They also crunch, not just the ground.

I hear that old familiar call,
Each time I leave, walk out the door,
"Be careful dear that you don't fall."
Those loving words I'll not ignore.

Some folks equate this final stage,
To winter months, leaves wither, die.
I'm blessed to reach this ripe old age.
It's not for me to question why.

Perhaps there's work remaining still.
God keeps me warm through winter's chill.

FEBRUARY 3, CALMING PRESENCE

As pellets catch the window's glow
A hint of dawn lights up the cloud.
The sleet gives way to falling snow,
Conceals the earth with icy shroud.

A peaceful scene as I awake,
A soothing sight that brings a smile.
The silence of each falling flake,
A calming presence for a while.

The stillness of dawn's early light,
A quiet place where peace is found.
Serenity when all seems right,
As snowflakes fall without a sound.

I pray like snow that inner peace
May still your soul, let joy increase.

FEBRUARY 4, GENTLE, STRONG

Lord help direct my words today.
It's not just things I long to do,
But also, what I choose to say,
That should align and both be true.

When I mess up, I make amends,
But can't erase the things I've said.
But words like kind and gentle friends
Can give encouragement and spread.

I pray for wisdom and control
Of words I use and what I say.
"Lift others up" should be my goal.
I pray that's true of me today.

Lord help me be both gentle, strong,
Share words that linger like a song.

FEBRUARY 5, DISCERNMENT

When I'm true to myself, who God made me to be,
Discover the talents created in me,
I find joy in perusing the things that I do,
Yet I'm open when God brings me something brand new.

I learn something new even times when I fail.
Perhaps an adventure along a new trail,
Perhaps it's a journey to places unknown.
Lord help me soar higher than I've ever flown.

Lord help me to follow wherever You lead.
Discern when to harvest or just plant a seed.
Help me avoid what can lead me astray.
Help me see clearly as You lead the way.

Lord grant me the wisdom to help me discern
What's next to discover, what's yet to be learned.

FEBRUARY 6, FINDING JOY

If I climbed every mountain, or learned how to fly,
Yet knew not the one who created the sky,
I'd keep looking and searching to find the next thrill,
Hoping to find it just over the hill.

There's always an ad for a new thing to try,
Offering something if only we'll buy,
Perhaps it is happiness, beauty, or fame.
In the end we find out that we're still just the same.

No human philosophy mankind provides
Can fulfill the longing for God that's inside.
Lord help me to see that I only need You.
In You I find rest, not in things that I do.

There's joy in the person of Jesus my King.
Lord You give me peace, with Your joy I can sing.

FEBRUARY 7, ENCOURAGEMENT

I pray the words I write ring true,
Provide encouragement to you.
I pray I touch a heart today,
By words I write, or share, or say.

I may not know the load you bear,
But pray my words convey I care.
It's often hard to see through pain,
Find rainbows after storms and rain.

I pray someday your heart can mend,
You too reach out to help a friend,
Find ways to lift someone in need,
A word, a gift, perhaps a deed.

I pray God's love I can impart.
His love can mend a broken heart.

FEBRUARY 8, HOW MANY?

If I sat down and had the time
How many sonnets could I rhyme?
Would it be more than just a few?
What would I write that's fresh and new?

If I just let my mind run free,
What's locked inside I need to see?
What's hidden there inside my mind?
How many verses could I find?

Would I find words that give us hope,
Provide the strength we need to cope?
I'll write the words while they still come,
And pray they find their way to some.

There may be times when there's no rain,
No words are flowing through my brain.

FEBRUARY 9, THE GREAT BEYOND

Beyond the realm of time and space
My soul will find its resting place,
United there with saints of old,
And beauty I can scarce behold.

I live this side of heaven's gate.
I do not know my final date,
Nor do I know my future here,
But trust the Lord and do not fear.

I long to see the great beyond
Embraced in love, no tighter bond.
Forever's just a breath away.
My earthly ties will fade away.

I'll understand and I'll know why
My future lies beyond the sky.

FEBRUARY 10, HERD IMMUNITY

Immunity combined with herd,
Quite common now to hear the word.
What once brought cattle, sheep to mind,
Now testing stations, cars in line.

Perceptions of the words have changed,
No longer picture open range.
We're grouped into a huddled mass.
Will we have changed once this has passed?

Have we become mere creatures now?
Are we less human, changed somehow?
No longer masked, we'll see each face.
Combined we form the human race.

We're more than beasts who roam the earth,
We each have spirit, soul at birth.
I pray we learn to love once more,
Show more compassion than before.

FEBRUARY 11, KINDNESS

We all can give others some kindness, respect,
A habit, when busy, we sometimes neglect.
It takes little effort, a nod or a smile.
When you give it a try you will find it worthwhile.

For someone in need, you can brighten their day.
It's amazing the kindness your words can convey.
It may be a stranger you pass on the street.
Perhaps it's a friend that you happen to meet.

Be careful the words that you use when you talk,
You don't know the pathway that others have walked.
Find ways to encourage with words from the heart.
Lift someone's spirit before you depart.

Some day when you're troubled, discouraged, or grieved,
I pray that same kindness is also received.

FEBRUARY 12, A SLOWER PACE

Some people like to rush about.
They always take the fastest route.
I much prefer a slower pace,
I don't consider life a race.

I like to savor days I live,
Find satisfaction when I give,
Find words to share from deep inside,
A place where peace and joy abide.

A quiet place for rhymes to form,
A resting place when life brings storms,
Provide me time to read and pray,
To contemplate just what to say.

I try to share with words I write,
God's perfect love, His peace, His Light.
The love of God found in His Word
Must be absorbed and not just heard.

FEBRUARY 13, TRUTH

It's hard to tolerate deceit.
I won't give up, accept defeat.
I'll seek the truth, ignore the lie,
So much to learn before I die.

When did we stray away from truth,
Declare integrity uncouth?
The pendulum has swung too far.
Deceit will smother us like tar.

I pray that lies will soon decease,
That honesty and truth increase.
I pray that words of truth take hold,
Become a treasure sought like gold.

Lord help us all to find a way
To spread the truth with words we say.

FEBRUARY 14, VALENTINE

Remember when in years gone by
We'd share our valentines with friends
To share our love or just say hi,
Perhaps with some to make amends.

Though older now we still need love.
I don't know who will read this card,
But share my love through God above.
I pray with love life's not so hard.

I pray through friends God sends His care,
The ones on whom you can depend,
Who gather 'round, they're always there,
The ones who'll always be your friend.

I pray your cherished friends are near.
Who share your journey, listen, hear.

FEBRUARY 15, TAKE TIME

I recommend some quiet time
   to let your soul find rest,
To give your spirit time to seek
   the pathway for your quest.
The journey through life's wilderness
   has many paths to choose.
Sometimes a pathway looks the same,
   it's easy to confuse.

The spirit deep inside our soul
   can help us each discern,
Discover what we're meant to do,
   the lessons we must learn.
We each have gifts, abilities,
   and talents we can share.
Don't let your talents go to waste,
   lay dormant, unaware.

Discover who you are inside,
   you truly are unique.
You may find traits and realize,
   you're more than you might think.
Sometimes we run through life too fast,
   don't take the time to seek
The yearnings deep within our soul,
   that have no voice to speak.

I pray each day you take the time
   to pause, reflect, and pray,
Discover all you're meant to be
   and do along the way.

FEBRUARY 16, SECRETS

If I could peer into your mind,
What's lurking there that I would find?
What stays inside you dare not share,
Keep those around you unaware?

If you keep secrets locked away,
When buried deep they rot, decay.
They eat away at heart and soul.
Confess your wrongs and be made whole.

Let light into that secret place.
Confront the secrets you must face.
Don't let the secrets stay inside,
Find someone close to trust, confide.

I pray you find a path that's right.
I pray your heart gives way to light.

FEBRUARY 17, THE ELDERLY

Those gentle winds of change each day,
That change us in such subtle ways,
Sometimes erupt as vicious storms,
Uproot our ways, traditions, norms.

A storm may leave our bodies frail.
We persevere, somehow prevail.
We learn as we encounter strife,
We make adjustments in our life.

Though not as young, or bold, or strong,
We still contribute, still belong.
Us elderly may need some care,
But still have much that we can share.

The wisdom gained by those now old
Is like a treasure chest of gold.

FEBRUARY 18, PRAYER AND CARE

For hurting friends, I say a prayer.
For those in need of tender care,
I pray that love will make its way
Into your heart and soul this day.

I pray that pain will fade, recede,
That doctors, nurses meet each need.
I pray that everyone you meet,
Helps lift you up back on your feet.

I pray that soon your strength returns.
Sometimes through hurts and pain we learn
The Lord through others in our life
Shows us His love in times of strife.

I pray you too can help a friend,
Be there for them until they mend.

FEBRUARY 19, WORD CHOICE

How many poems will I write?
Which words will I allow to soar?
Who am I to give them flight,
Leave other words that I ignore?

So many ways to turn a phrase,
So many words from which to choose,
Sometimes the words form through a haze,
Which words will win while others lose?

It's not a battle that they fought.
I just pick one that fits the best,
That paints the picture of the thought,
The rhythm is the final test.

I try to find the words to say
What's in my heart and soul each day.

FEBRUARY 20, SOCIAL DISTANCE

Where is the hug, the warm embrace,
The kiss placed softly on my face?
Is social distance here to stay?
It sends a message, "Stay away."

Reach out to hold or shake a hand,
Says "I am here, I understand."
There's healing in the human touch,
Conveying love we need so much.

I pray as we begin to heal
We still express the way we feel,
Once more use touch to show we care,
A warm embrace or hug to share.

I pray when others gather near
There'll be no wall or veil of fear.

FEBRUARY 21, I FOLLOW

When life's a mess, things go awry,
When I can't find the reasons why,
I realize God's in control.
Whate'er He chooses will unfold.

I yield to Him, His master plan.
My life He holds within His hand.
He needs no one to ask, consult,
He knows the final end result.

God's in control, my future, past,
What matters most, the things that last.
I cannot fathom, understand
His universe, so vast, so grand.

God doesn't answer to my whim.
He's in control, I follow Him.

FEBRUARY 22, A FRIEND'S COMFORT

Perhaps you're the one who needs comfort today,
Or perhaps it's another you help in some way.
We all need each other. We all need a friend.
Someone beside us to help us to mend.

Those times when we're hurting, feel helpless and lost,
Our friendships are priceless, not measured by cost.
We need someone beside us with whom we can share
Who'll soothe as they listen, give comfort and care.

Whether you or a friend is the one who's in need,
Either give or receive a kind word or a deed.
Those times when we're hurting, we also will learn
The value of comfort that we can return.

I know that no matter what you're going through
The Lord is a friend who'll bring comfort to you.

FEBRUARY 23, HOW TO SHARE

If my rhymes are just read, only heard by a few,
Lord give me the wisdom to know what to do.
I don't try to hide them beneath a big rock.
Is it time to slow down, reassess, and take stock?

Are the rhymes that I pen just a journal for me?
Should I really be sharing them, setting them free?
Should I still keep on reading, recording my sound?
If I read them aloud will a few gather 'round?

It does my heart good to write verses in rhyme.
Perhaps it's too often, one poem at a time,
To share what I write and each verse I compose,
Instead, a bouquet, not just one single rose.

I'll continue to write, and to read, and to pray,
I'll seek the Lord's guidance to show me the way.

FEBRUARY 24, JOURNAL PAGES

Is this a day without a rhyme?
There is no law. It's not a crime.
Why do I feel a need to share
My thoughts and feelings, joys and cares?

Should journal pages be unlocked,
Exposed to probing eyes, or blocked?
To open up, let others see
My heart and soul helps set me free.

The good, the bad, the new, the old
All part of me inside my soul.
I could just let them stay and hide
Just hibernate and stay inside.

If I share thoughts as they appear
Perhaps someone will read or hear,
Some kindred spirit will relate,
Let in God's love and end the hate.

The words I write and share I pray
Help others seek and find their way.

FEBRUARY 25, QUIET MORNINGS

It's now been countless years ago
When in my teens, much yet to know,
We had a place, small getaway,
There on the lake weekends we'd stay.

Behind the boat I loved to ski.
The times back then seemed so carefree.
The thrill of speeding 'cross the waves
Now memories forever saved.

Although the skis gave me a thrill
I also savored quiet, still.
The early morning dawning sky,
Times spent with Dad for fish to fry.

Those quiet mornings in the boat
A sheltered place, tie up, just float.
A rod, a bob, a hook with bait,
Throw out the line, sit back and wait.

Those quiet mornings spent with Dad
I learned to cherish as a lad.

FEBRUARY 26, CHILDHOOD FRIENDS

The friends I knew at early age
Helped write my life, they're on each page.
They each became a part of me,
We're intertwined, will always be.

Sometimes we fought, but mostly played.
The lessons learned began first grade.
Throughout the years our friendships grew.
Those ties still last that we once knew.

The plays we ran while on the field
Taught us to stand, and not to yield,
Together learned to fight and win,
Helped us transition, boys to men.

I'm grateful for the girls I met.
I learned respect, I've no regrets.
They formed in me a special place
For tenderness, a warm embrace.

Those memories formed as a child,
They're part of me, still bring a smile.

FEBRUARY 27, HEROIC ACTS

Heroic acts inside Ukraine
Will be remembered, not in vain.
It's time to rally, help our friends,
They have a nation to defend.

Throughout the world instilling pride,
Let's let them know we're on their side.
It's time to let the villains know
That they will reap just what they sow.

It's time to stand, to show we're strong,
United join in freedom's song.
We stand together, raise our voice,
Let evil know we've made our choice.

No matter what may be their fate,
They took a stand to end the hate,
Forever know in history
As ones who fought, remaining free.

Let's pray for those who stand and fight.
It's time for wrongs to be made right.

FEBRUARY 28, MY REFLECTION

I'm not yet old inside my head.
It's just the mirror that I dread.
The face that's looking back at me
Is showing age I must agree.

I'm grateful for my hair, though white.
Some lose it all, someday I might.
I'm getting wrinkles, quite a few,
I must admit, I'm not brand new.

I pray each day I've yet to live
I find I've something still to give.
As long as I can write and care,
I pray I'm blessed with words to share.

I pray for words that offer hope,
Will touch a heart, help someone cope.

MARCH 1, FOCUS MY THOUGHTS

It's easy to find all the wrong that's around.
It's on the news daily and easily found.
I pray I'm not jaded, persuaded each day
To look at the world in a cynical way.

If I focus my thoughts on the things that are true,
Then the clouds fade away and the sky turns to blue.
If I'm fixed on the lovely, what's pure and what's right,
Then the Lord brings me peace as I walk in His light.

I'm not one to ignore or pretend there's no wrong,
But I must keep a balance, sing praise with a song.
The Lord gives me strength and the faith that I need
To follow Him daily, perhaps plant a seed.

I trust in the Lord as I lift up my prayer.
In Him I find peace and a love I can share.

MARCH 2, BUSY MORN

A busy morn, a busy week,
That bit of quiet time I seek
May get cut short but can't resist.
To share with rhyme for me is bliss.

To share in rhyme a word or two,
Perhaps today just pen a few,
It helps my heart and brain survive
Like bees returning to the hive.

I'm not quite sure just why I share.
If someone asks me how or where
I get the words I pen each day.
I never know quite what to say.

As best I know and can explain,
God reached inside and lit a flame.

MARCH 3, DAILY PRAYER

Dear Lord, I come in prayer to You.
I pray the words I pen are true.
I pray they're pleasing in Your sight.
Lord help me spread Your perfect light.

Instill Your love and peace in me,
Help spread the news, You set us free.
We each can have a change of heart,
Find lasting love that won't depart.

You paid the price for every sin.
I now look up, not where I've been.
Your words are fresh and new each day.
Lord help me see what they convey.

Instill in me the will to learn
And wisdom needed to discern.

MARCH 4, WORDS SHARED

The words I place upon the page
Don't ask about degrees or age,
If I'm a novice or a sage,
Just if the words I share are true.

Words can be twisted, made to lie.
I'm always careful, always try,
Make sure my words don't go awry,
Just keep them honest, fresh, and new.

Will words be loving, gentle, kind
Inside this body, soul, and mind?
What's undiscovered still to find?
Perhaps some seeds took root and grew.

I pray the words that I accrue
Will lift your heart when shared with you.

MARCH 5, MY ROLE

God bless the ones that I may reach.
May words I write inspire and teach.
I've not set out to reach some goal,
It seems, for now, to write's my role.

If you're in need of prayer today,
God knows your need, for you I pray.
I pray your hope and faith increase.
I pray you find His perfect peace.

For those confused, depressed, or down,
I pray what's lost will soon be found.
I pray your soul will clearly see
Who God created you to be.

God's Spirit reaches out to you.
Embrace God's love that's pure and true.

MARCH 6, REMAINING DAYS

Lord help me use my time on earth,
May I be faithful day by day,
Pursue the things of lasting worth,
Reflect Your love with words I say.

May Your love grow inside of me,
Sink deep its roots, find fertile ground,
Tame evil ways and set me free
To hear Your voice, how sweet the sound.

Lord help me find the words of praise
To lift You up, reveal Your love
With all of my remaining days,
Until I'm home with You above.

May others hear my words, my song,
Be drawn to You, know they belong.

MARCH 7, NEVER MUNDANE

Has life become routine, mundane,
  and every day's the same?
Don't let the rut obscure the view,
  a burning bush aflame.
It shouldn't take a big event
  to turn to God and pray,
I much prefer to read His word
  and talk with Him each day.

I pray my daily walk with God
  will never be mundane.
Lord keep my verses fresh and new,
  when writing each refrain.
Lord keep my mind, my thoughts, my prayers,
  just focusing on You,
Help me reflect with words I pen,
  Your love that's pure and true.

I've never seen a burning bush,
  I likely never will,
But even in my golden years
  I know You're with me still.
Each day I read, I pray, I write
  my simple lines in rhyme.
I trust You Lord if there's a change,
  another hill to climb.

You've blessed me Lord and led the way.
   You've guided me in life.
You've led me to the mountain tops.
   You've walked with me through strife.
I trust You Lord to lead me now,
   I pray I finish well.
I have more verses left to write,
   more stories left to tell.

MARCH 8, LIFE CHANGES

My life is a book penned one line at a time.
Sometimes it makes sense, and the lines seem to rhyme.
Sometimes out of focus the lines seem to blur.
It's hard to predict what's about to occur.

Circumstances may change and can turn on a dime.
I don't get to choose them, the place, or the time.
I learn to adjust to the rhythm of life,
A mixture of laughter, adventure, and strife.

Life's always changing, it's stranger each day.
What comes in the future is not mine to say.
Life is not something that I understand,
Each day that's ahead I just place in God's hand.

I pray for the courage to learn to embrace
Whatever befalls me each day I must face.

MARCH 9, RUBBISH

What enters my senses comes in from outside.
I have some control what's allowed to abide.
What stays for a while as I ponder and think
Can show me new heights or form cesspools that stink.

If I filter what enters and stays in my mind,
I'm less prone to evil, perhaps even kind.
With so many around me to lead me astray,
I need every morning to read and to pray,

To sift through the rubble inside of my brain,
Hang on to the treasures, remove what brings pain.
When I toss it out early, don't let it take hold,
It's my way of guarding my heart and my soul.

I pray for the wisdom to know what to keep
Get rid of the rubbish I stack in a heap.

MARCH 10, BE BLESSED

If I write from my heart as I'm reading God's word
And put into rhyme what for me I have heard,
Should my writings be private, or something I share?
Perhaps they'll touch someone when I'm not aware.

I won't dwell on discouragement, how I might feel.
It's God I am serving, it's His love that's real.
No matter what others may happen to say,
It's for God I am writing and sharing this way.

I'll continue to share with the words that I write.
Perhaps I'll help others be drawn to the light.
My words help express what I find in God's word.
There will always be scoffers who say they're absurd.

I pray there are some who find comfort and rest,
Are led to know Jesus and truly are blessed.

MARCH 11, A PAUSE

I'm grateful for a place that's warm,
A place to shelter from the storm.
Some days I'm better off inside,
A time to rest and just abide.

So many years I had to rush.
I savor silent, quiet hush.
No looming deadline left to meet,
Another project to complete.

Those years back then they call my prime,
So much to do, so little time.
I've entered now my golden years,
My pace has switched to lower gears.

Perhaps this phase will be my prime.
Some days I seem to have more time.
I get to choose the things I do.
Take time to focus on a few.

I now have time to contemplate,
Write down my thoughts, they'll come, I wait.
Perhaps there's someone else in need
Who'll take the time to pause and read,

Find comfort in the words I write,
Peer through the darkness, find the light.

MARCH 12, EXPRESSIONS OF LOVE

Our daughter's now grown, and her kids are grown too.
She's become a proud grandmother, one and then two.
Life passes quickly, the weeks become years.
Cherish the moments with loved ones so dear.

Though I've built up a lifetime of love in my heart,
I must show and express it before I depart.
What good is my love if it's never made known,
If my love's never spoken or even been shown?

I pray that I'm faithful to share what I feel,
Take time to be genuine, tender, and real.
Expressions of love seem to last a long time,
Even the simple ones written in rhyme.

I pray that the verses I write every day
Help others find love that they too can convey.

MARCH 13, SHARED WORDS

If I shared from my heart, allowed others to look,
If I captured my words to be read in a book,
Would anyone care about my point of view,
An old man with grey hair, it's not like I'm brand new.

Perhaps if I write from my heart and I share,
Open up and give others a glimpse what is there,
That by sharing my words and not choosing to hide,
Others are touched as they're peering inside.

With so many memories I've tucked away,
I can't keep them all buried to rot and decay.
Perhaps it's just something folks do at this stage,
Share from the heart writing page after page.

I pray that the books that I write will survive;
A few even read them while I'm still alive.

MARCH 14, PRAY EVERY DAY

I pray daily for loved ones, for family, for friends.
I pray for God's wisdom in words that I pen.
I pray for God's blessings each day as I write.
I pray as I share, I point others toward light.

Why carry the burdens that life brings my way?
I can ask for God's help if I take time to pray.
It's not fancy words, or the way that I speak,
He hears when I'm weary, I'm down, or I'm weak.

I also share praises, give thanks to the Lord,
Let Him know I am grateful, how much He's adored.
He knows me completely, He hears every prayer.
I'm amazed how He loves me and wants me to share.

Lord I'm grateful You listen, You know, and You hear.
In You I find peace, I have nothing to fear.

MARCH 15, A PRAYER

Lord grace me with wisdom to know how to pray,
To know others' needs, how to help in some way.
Prayer makes a difference, I don't know just how,
But I count an honor and come to You now.

Lord I lift those now hurting, the ones that I know.
I pray for Your touch, set their spirit aglow.
I also lift others perhaps I've not met.
I pray they find comfort, know you've paid their debt.

I also give thanks for things that You do,
How You loved me at times I was blind, never knew.
You guided my life, led me down every trail.
I learned how to pray, know without You I'd fail.

You know every need, yet You still want to hear
Our prayers for each other, for those we hold dear.

MARCH 16, TIME TO TURN

Our bodies grow fragile, our minds become weak.
The greatest among us can't give what we seek.
We long for the reasons, the answers to why.
We all know for certain this body will die.

Wars rage around us the rockets like rain
Bringing down misery, heartache, and pain.
Evil walks proudly how long can it last?
Where is the honor we've known in the past?

So many are biased, push their point of view.
The number we trust has now shrunk to a few.
It's time to acknowledge that God's in control.
He is the One we can trust with our soul.

It's time to seek answers from God as we pray.
Acknowledge that He is the truth and the way.

MARCH 17, HONORING A FRIEND

We honor you friend on this day of your birth.
We're blessed to be with you, a servant of worth.
You've touched many lives, you are faithful to pray,
Helped the sick and afflicted in your special way.

God's Spirit is in you, you're loving and kind,
Your gentle compassion, a gem, a rare find.
You know how to laugh, and you bring us good cheer.
You share words of wisdom that we need to hear.

We're blessed by your presence, you make the room bright,
A man of integrity sharing God's light.
You've served the Lord faithfully down through the years.
Your kind gentle spirit has calmed many fears.

We're blessed to be with you, to call you a friend.
You're blessed by the Lord, and His love never ends.

MARCH 18, SET APART

Magnificent beauty created by God,
Eruptions in springtime come forth from a pod.
We hear the birds singing, they soar through the sky.
God gave them wings and He made them to fly.

Thousands of creatures inhabit the earth,
Each with a span that begins with a birth.
We all share a planet that circles the sun.
Understanding the vastness has only begun.

What makes humans different? We all have a heart.
What is unique that sets mankind apart?
God gave us His spirit, we long to be whole.
God placed eternity deep in our soul.

God gave me the faith that eternity's real.
One day I will see Him, His glory revealed.

MARCH 19, ONE IN A CROWD

I'm only one voice that gets lost in a crowd.
The news seems more violent, piercing, and loud.
It seems that the loudest just want to be heard,
But their message, preposterous, downright absurd.

Yet they gather a following, others agree.
The truth is ignored though it's easy to see.
How can so many just follow along?
Perhaps by agreeing they think they belong.

If a few speak the truth can a nation be turned?
Can the lessons from history ever be learned?
If we lose faith in God and we think we know best,
Think we have earned it, deny we've been blessed,

We'll be choosing a path that's been taken before.
I pray we are spared, seek His blessings once more.

MARCH 20, CUP OF JOE

Why is it called a cup of Joe,
This morning coffee that I drink?
It came about so long ago,
No one's for sure just what they think.

Some say Joe's short for Java bean
Throw in some Mocha, form jamoke.
On this idea some aren't too keen,
Think Joe refers to common folks.

The term is old, before my time
But what I do remember still,
A cup of coffee for a dime,
Good conversation, free refills.

Although those days have long since passed,
Fond memories will always last.

MARCH 21, GOD'S GIFT

I know Your truth will set me free
To be a better form of me.
I pray for inward strength, resolve,
Whatever change that may involve.

I pray that as I read and learn
Inside my heart I can discern
Your Holy Spirit from above
Instructing me in truth and love.

I cannot buy, nor can I hire
A way to fill my heart's desire.
Your love's a gift I just receive.
A greater gift I can't conceive.

Lord help me share your love today,
With words I write and words I say.

MARCH 22, EMBRACE

We all are a part of just one human race.
We all need each other to hold and embrace.
Contact with others, restricted these days,
Has brought about changes, in so many ways.

What will it do to our long-term existence,
If children are taught to maintain social distance?
Not sure I can tolerate life without touch.
I'm missing the contact I value so much.

I often now hesitate, "Fist bump or shake?"
Asking "Are hugs worth the risk that I take?"
I'm weary of distancing six feet apart.
It's hard to communicate, share from the heart.

Until we're no longer in fear of a bug
I offer my words as a virtual hug.

MARCH 23, AN OLD MAN AND HIS BLANKET

He sat in his rocker and jotted down words,
A blanket to cover him, ward off the cold.
He wrote of his life and the things he had heard.
His years were approaching what some would call old.

He penned all the memories down through the years,
Some mem'ries of childhood when he was a boy,
Some not so happy, his words came with tears,
Others quite pleasant he shared with great joy.

He was blessed on his journey, he walked with the Lord.
He was able to share it, God gave him a wife.
Together in harmony each played a chord,
God answered his prayers with the love of his life.

Though never quite certain why he loved to write
Or where words would take him or where they might go,
As he began writing in dawn's early light,
That time before sunrise when colors would glow.

The old man with his blanket still rocks, spinning rhyme.
He writes about life as he walks back through time.

MARCH 24, READ AND PRAY

If I read the Bible and earnestly pray,
Your scriptures will guide me and show me the way.
They give me discernment the things I should know,
Provide me direction, which way I should go.

Your Spirit will help me to see, understand
The words You provided, recorded by hand.
Passed down through the ages they're meaningful, true,
Each time that I read them I see something new.

Your Spirit is with me, I'm never alone.
I don't need Your number to text or to phone.
Your Spirit inside me sent down from above
Provides me assurance I'm wrapped in Your love.

I'm grateful for those who recorded Your Word.
You guided their hand as they wrote what they heard.

MARCH 25, PURPOSE AND WORTH

I'm not able to function in life all alone,
Don't claim to be prefect in all that I do.
I'm only a person, some flesh and some bone.
I'm no master of trades, only skilled at a few.

I'm dependent on others around me each day
For food that I eat, even clothes that I buy,
All working together, each earning their pay.
I can't do it all and I don't even try.

We all are quite different in how we are made.
Some are quite gifted in music or art.
Some pursue science, and others a trade.
We each have a role and we each form a part.

We each have a place on this planet called earth.
We each one have value, and purpose, and worth.

MARCH 26, EACH SEASON

We mark our life in years not days.
We measure seasons of our lives.
When looking back we see each phase.
At times we struggle to survive.

I'm grateful Lord that I can pray.
You listen Lord. You hear each prayer.
You give me strength I need today.
I need Your love. I know You care.

You're always there to get me through.
When I'm in need You comfort me.
I read Your Word, I know it's true.
Lord help my heart and soul to see.

Today's brand new, the sun will rise.
Help me become each day more wise.

MARCH 27, WALKING BY FAITH

God placed eternity deep in our souls.
We're all seeking something to fill a vast void.
It's only through Jesus that we are made whole.
Our souls will persist, something we'll not avoid.

If we walk with Lord and in Him place our trust,
His Spirit will lead us and guide us in truth.
We seek after treasure that never will rust
By walking in faith, not insisting on proof.

Satan's a counterfeit, tries to persuade,
By twisting and spinning what man can conceive.
He's not a creator, there's nothing he's made.
He recycles man's lies and he tries to deceive.

God gives us the answers, we learn from His word,
Discerning the truth to expose the absurd.

MARCH 28, CONTENT

I'll never write a masterpiece,
Or win a Nobel prize for peace.
My books won't make the New York Times.
I'm quite content to weave my rhymes.

I write to soothe, to feel less stressed,
Words help my soul find quiet rest.
The words I write I often share
Perhaps touch someone unaware,

Someone perhaps I'll never meet,
Won't have the chance to hug and greet.
I pray my words help ease their mind.
Take time to pause, reflect, unwind.

This life is not a sprint to race,
Does not demand a frantic pace.

MARCH 29, PRAISE HIM

We lift up our voices Lord praising your name.
You are worthy oh Lord to receive all our praise.
That's why we are here, it's the reason we came.
Your love is forever, not measured in days.

You came as a man made of flesh and of bone.
The angels sang praises as Mary gave birth.
There's no greater love that has ever been known.
Your power and majesty permeate earth.

Your name is the sweetest that we'll ever hear,
You are the Holy one, God's only Son,
A name angels praise and one demons all fear.
With glory and honor You fought, and You won.

We lift up our voices with angels we sing.
We offer in song all the praises we bring.

MARCH 30, FIND PEACE

When I focus on things in my life I control,
Instead of the things in the world I can't change,
I'm able to rest and find peace in my soul,
Stay focused on things that I can rearrange.

I can share what I've learned in my years on this earth.
I can write about life and the things that I see.
I can tell someone else they have value and worth.
But I can't force another to learn it from me.

We each have a past and a future to live.
We each form opinions, have something to say.
We each have a talent and something to give.
I pray I help someone who's searching today.

I pray they find answers. They're found in God's word.
His words offer peace like no others I've heard.

MARCH 31, GOOD NEWS

Lord guide my path, my words, my tongue,
Help others find Your love, Your light,
Tell of Your grace to old and young,
Spread Your good news with what I write.

You came to earth that we might live.
You gave Your life. Your Word is true.
The only Son God had to give,
A sacrifice for me, for you.

He died and rose, He conquered death.
He offers life, His love is real.
He gives to me my every breath.
Forevermore my future's sealed.

In simple faith reach out in prayer.
With open arms, He'll meet you there.

APRIL 1, A COUNTRY SONG

If I could write a country song
I'd pen a tune that's smooth and long
Share what I know, not hesitate,
That true love's real and worth the wait

I'd write of love that's strong and true
I'd play a melody for you
Of love that's grown through many years
A love that lasts through joy and tears

Just watch the birds glide through the sky
See beauty in a butterfly
Allow your heart to sing along
You'll find true love it won't be long

Just take it slow don't go too fast
It takes some work to make it last
In love commitment is the key
For love to flourish, healthy, free

I'd play that song around the world
To every boy and every girl
Let others know the way I feel
I'd share with them that love is real

APRIL 2, NOT ALONE

If I lived on an island, was stranded alone,
Would I survive? Would my heart turn to stone?
Could I live without friends who provide love and care?
I'm not meant for an island with no one to share.

My friends share the good times, rejoice when I'm glad.
They're with me in sorrow whenever I'm sad.
My friends give encouragement, help me survive.
Refreshed by their friendship I'm fully alive.

Surrounded by friends I find comfort and hope.
The prayers of my friends lift me up, help me cope.
The Lord is our hope, and we all share His love.
Our hope is in glory, our home is above.

I pray that I too am considered a friend,
Return every kindness, help others to mend.

APRIL 3, GRAND AT FIFTY
(For my daughter on her birthday)

It doesn't seem so long ago
I'd brush your hair and tie a bow.
So many memories we share,
We gave to you our love and care.

We loved to camp in RV parks,
Enjoy the campfire after dark,
Sing silly songs, invent a word,
Though some made sense, most were absurd.

You grew in body, mind and soul,
High intellect and heart of gold.
You made us proud by standing strong,
Help others feel that they belong.

You raised three children of your own,
Helped each mature, now they are grown.
Two now are parents, twice you're grand,
Two little girls, each in good hands.

Five decades come and go so fast,
So many days now in your past,
So many more yet to unfold,
Your heart and soul are never old.

APRIL 4, BEFORE DAWN

The stars are still shining, the contrast is stark.
Their light brings such beauty, the night is so dark.
So quiet and peaceful that time before dawn,
I savor the stillness before it is gone.

As I pause to reflect on how vast His domain,
Too awesome's my God for my mind to contain.
How can I fathom the heavens above,
Or understand fully the depths of His love?

The darkness will fade as it yields to the light,
When God once again brings an end to the night.
I take time to reflect, know that God's in control.
God understands me, mind, body, and soul.

No matter the depth of my troubles each day,
The Lord is beside me to show me the way.

APRIL 5, WILL IT END?

When I think about stopping this writing in rhyme,
Consider what else I should do with that time,
I ask if they truly have value or worth,
These verses that form as I give the words birth.

The verses keep forming inside of my brain.
I jot them all down as I write each refrain.
I wonder if ever this rhyming will end.
How long will they linger these verses I've penned?

As the words come together, form verses and flow,
I pray they fall quietly, gently like snow.
I pray like a lullaby soothes a small child,
My words offer comfort, bring peace for a while.

As long as words come, it's my pleasure to write,
Watch them soar through the air as the verses take flight.

APRIL 6, ALWAYS THERE

Will anyone hear what I say
With words I pen most every day?
What should I share, what should I hide,
When I peer deep to look inside?

If I should share, let others peek
Will they find answers that they seek?
Will they find solace when they know,
My ducks are never in a row?

We all face struggles in this life.
We all go through some times of strife.
I know those times can make me strong,
Yet pray those days won't stay for long.

I've learned one thing I know is true.
The Lord will always help me through.
He's always there. He's my best friend,
Beyond the time when this life ends.

APRIL 7, DAILY FEAST

I love stillness of mornings, the quiet, the calm.
I find comfort in scriptures, a Proverb or Psalm.
A time to reflect on what God has to say.
A needed transition from nighttime to day.

Though the Bible is ancient and centuries old,
It still contains wisdom more precious than gold.
God's words are refreshing, each day something new,
There's always more wisdom I need to accrue.

It's a blessing to read and to feast on His word,
Take time to absorb all I've read, and I've heard.
The moments I'm spending each morning in prayer,
Draw me toward heaven, and help me prepare

For the day that I see Him and look in His face.
I'll dwell with Him there. He's prepared me a place.

APRIL 8, ALONE NOT FORGOTTEN

Find someone who's lonely, in need of a friend.
Ignored and forgotten it's easy to hide.
An invisible curtain begins to descend,
With no one to listen, just sadness inside.

If someone seems different and not like the rest,
It's easy to turn and pretend they're not there.
Someone hurting in silence won't likely protest,
Just continue assuming there's no one to care.

Perhaps it's some tragedy early in life,
That began a long journey of feeling alone.
If their shell is too thick to cut through with a knife,
Don't assume that inside is a heart made of stone.

Lord open my heart help me see through Your eyes,
Help me to hear those who silently cry.

APRIL 9, JUDGE NOT

If I don't know the path that you've trod,
Nor walked in your shoes, not a step,
Then I've no right to think you are odd,
Or consider your actions inept.

Perhaps you've survived many trials,
That would cause many others to fail.
It's remarkable you can still smile,
When others would cry, even wail.

I hate to hear others complain
About how someone else should behave.
We all are a tad bit insane,
Even more as we're nearer our grave.

I'll take a deep breath and relax,
Judge not without all of the facts.

APRIL 10, THE WELL

For me to write and share in rhyme
Is more than how I pass the time.
It soothes the soul inside of me
To liberate and set words free.

Not sure I know the reason why,
Or when and if the well runs dry,
Nor understand why I'm compelled
To share the words drawn from that well.

Each time the bucket on the rope
Comes up I pray it offers hope.
I pray the water's clear and pure,
Gives others strength helps them endure.

We all get thirsty on the trail,
Begin to fear that we might fail,
Need time to rest restore the soul,
Evaluate what is our goal.

I pray your soul is lifted up,
You know the One who fills my cup.
I pray you know the Prince of Peace,
Whose living waters never cease.

APRIL 11, SIN NATURE

Verbal incontinence, dribbles and drips,
Words flushed through the mouth and then out
  through the lips.
Not every thought that takes form in the brain
Should always be uttered, we learn to refrain.

Words can be raw with no form of restraint.
Good artists take time before touching the paint.
Something once beautiful brought forth a smile,
But twisted by Satan becomes something vile.

Sin passed down from Adam still plagues us today,
Internal urges to have it our way.
We think we know best and pursue our own plan.
We learn to ignore and resist God's commands.

Sin has invaded with trouble and strife,
But sin was defeated, God's Son gave His life.

APRIL 12, IN TIMES OF GRIEF

In times when we're hurting and suffer in grief,
Surrounded by others yet empty inside,
We're searching for comfort, in need of relief,
Our grief after loss will take time to subside.

Our loss leaves a hole that's not easy to fill.
Perhaps it's a parent, a sibling or child,
Or even a job where we practiced a skill.
Whether sudden or something we knew for a while,

The loss, like a dream, is still hard to believe.
The grief is still deep, and the wounds are still there.
Some may need solitude, quiet to grieve,
Others need friends to surround them with care.

I pray through the words you will feel my embrace,
That they bring you some comfort as healing takes place.

APRIL 13, LEARNING TO GIVE

Our life here is short and it soon will be gone.
Life is more about giving than what we accrue.
Our life's but an instant, we soon will move on.
That our life here will end we all know to be true.

We came here with nothing, that's how we will leave.
We mature while we're here as we learn how to give.
Those we have known, for a time they will grieve,
But each will continue to breathe and to live.

What I give of myself in the days I'm alive
Can survive when I'm gone if I choose to let go.
I pray what I leave can continue and thrive,
Love shared from the heart can continue to grow.

Lord help me find something to give every day,
Leave something of value though I cannot stay.

APRIL 14, AFTER THE STORM

A beautiful sunrise that follows a storm,
Clouds painted with colors with dawn's early glow,
With sun on my face, I feel cozy and warm.
The winds have subsided and no longer blow.

Serenaded by birds who are sharing in song,
The morning brings peace after storms through the night.
The winds and the rain can at times become strong,
With rumbles of thunder and flashes of light.

Sometimes it takes storms to find peace for a while,
Let go of the notion that we're in control,
The call of an eagle, the laugh of a child,
The sounds of tranquility, peace in the soul.

I pray that your journey includes times to rest,
Times to see beauty, count ways you've been blessed.

APRIL 15, GIVE PRAISE

If I were a flower that blooms in the spring,
I would praise my creator to Him I would sing.

If I were a mountain I'd reach to the sky
I'd give God the glory and praise Him on high.

If I were an ocean or even a sea,
I'd praise God for the life that is teeming in me.

If I were a tree I would offer my fruits,
As a praise to the God who gives strength to my roots.

If I were a cluster of grapes on the vine,
I would offer myself to my God for fine wine.

If I were a gem stone asleep in the night,
I'd praise God every morning reflecting His light.

All God's creations know how they were made.
They know their creator the memory won't fade.

He gave us dominion o'er all of the earth.
Why don't we all praise Him who formed us at birth?

APRIL 16, SIMPLE GESTURES

If I'm constantly looking for something brand new,
Something grand, something large, I might overlook small.
It's not about grandeur or what I accrue,
If my life's void of love, then I've nothing at all.

Sometimes it's the smallest of things that I give.
Simple gestures of love often do the most good.
I'm not measured by wealth but the way that I live.
Without love a hard heart becomes petrified wood.

As I'm watching and waiting and looking for ways
To reach out to others through words that I write,
Then I pray I help others and brighten their days
By sharing God's love and reflecting His light.

I find satisfaction in simple and plain.
I pray I share love as I pen each refrain.

APRIL 17, BITS AND PIECES

A snuggled down Lucy asleep in my lap
A time to curl up and to finish her nap.
As I sip on my coffee and stroke her soft fur
I capture my thoughts as they stretch, and they stir.

The patio's wet, the clouds hinting of rain
May water my words as I write each refrain.
My thoughts don't much matter, I just love to write.
I guess in a small way I try to spread light.

If I share a small piece of myself every day
Perhaps someone else will be touched in some way.
It's not easy to share, to come out of my shell,
But I jot down my thoughts, send them off, wish them well.

It's my way of giving and leaving behind
Small bits of my heart, and my soul, and my mind.

APRIL 18, GOD'S GIFTS

Endowed with gifts bestowed at birth,
It's up to us to find their worth.
Some talents dormant through the years
Await the time when they appear.

We did not choose the time or place,
But gifts emerged, we got a taste.
We found it sweet when first we tried.
It touched our soul, it satisfied.

We each bring gifts before the Lord,
Not gifts we buy or can afford,
But rather gifts shared from our heart,
God given gifts that won't depart.

I pray God's gifts, at least a few,
Have blessed your life and others too.

APRIL 19, A CUP AND A FRIEND

It's nice to have some time to think,
Some solitude to sit and be.
But also, nice to share a drink,
Some coffee or a cup of tea,

With those we love, converse aloud,
Share stories of those yesteryears
When we were young and strong and proud,
Those memories that we hold dear.

Though through the years some friendships fade,
Lose track of those that we once knew,
As we share love, new friends are made.
We all could add at least a few.

I pray you'll always have a friend,
Someone on whom you can depend.

APRIL 20, GARDENERS

Our children grow, we lend a hand,
To help them grow the best we can.
We till the garden, plant the seeds,
We keep it watered, free of weeds.

We watch them sprout, break through the ground,
Begin to see and look around.
As tiny leaves begin to form,
They need the light to keep them warm.

Their roots reach deep into the soil.
We know each one is worth the toil.
The spring brings rain with wind and storm.
We see the buds begin to form.

We see them bloom, grow strong, mature.
We're confident they will endure.

APRIL 21, NO PERFECT RHYME

I long to write the perfect rhyme
With words combined in perfect style,
Whose lyrics pass the test of time,
Allow a wounded heart to smile

With words that form inside my heart,
That paint a picture clear and pure,
To touch the soul, a work of art
That penetrates to last, endure.

I know my words are simple, plain,
Not seen by many eyes at all.
I must admit they're quite mundane,
Not likely mounted on a wall.

I'm satisfied to touch a few,
Spread hope and love like morning dew.

APRIL 22, DAYS OF SPRING

The winds for days blew loud and strong,
And after darkness all night long.
But morning breaks with calm and still.
A hint of gentle breeze I feel.

The scent of flowers in the air,
A fragrance that they gladly share.
There on the branch a small cocoon,
A butterfly emerging soon.

These cherished moments, tastes of spring,
Sweet echoes from the past they bring.
My younger self spread on the grass
Observing clouds to watch them pass.

The days of leisure as a child,
Remembering still brings a smile.

APRIL 23, GUIDE ME

I don't have all the answers yet
To what my life is all about.
About as close as I can get
Is read God's word when I'm in doubt.

So many twists and turns these days,
With many changes in the air,
When life's like walking in a haze
I lift my voice to God in prayer.

When I'm confused, don't understand,
When troubles press on every side,
I feel the warmth, God's outstretched hand.
I trust in Him to lead and guide.

Lord thank You for Your love each day,
For helping me to find my way.

APRIL 24, FIND JOY

We're frail and we're human. We're made out of clay.
Our Father's in heaven, we're children of light.
We think we are strong, and we wander astray.
We escape under darkness, the cover of night.

Why the attraction of evil and harm?
What's so alluring that pulls us to choose
Evil not virtue? I don't see the charm.
It's a path to destruction there's so much to lose.

What good is a mountain of silver or gold,
Or a room full of trophies and plaques and awards,
If you gain the whole world and you give up your soul?
Life's full of illusions that shatter in shards.

Our Father is waiting in heaven above.
May our hearts fill with joy from the true source of love.

APRIL 25, EACH DAY

We mark our life in years not days.
We measure seasons of our lives.
When looking back we see each phase.
At times we struggle to survive.

I'm grateful Lord that I can pray.
You listen Lord. You hear each prayer.
You give me strength I need today.
I need Your love. I know You care.

You're always there to get me through.
When I'm in need You comfort me.
I read Your Word, I know it's true.
Lord help my heart and soul to see.

Today's brand new, the sun will rise.
Help me become each day more wise.

APRIL 26, A MARATHON

When young I rushed like life's a race,
But realized in later days,
A marathon is more life's pace.
I see it more each passing phase.

It's not about how fast I run,
About the places I have sailed,
Or even parties, having fun.
There's more to life beyond the veil.

Our life is more than time on earth.
Our time is but a whisper here.
The clock begins to mark our birth.
Beyond the grave is not to fear.

The Lord said come, there's so much more.
Can't wait to see beyond the door.

APRIL 27, THOSE WHO SOAR

It once was easy to declare,
"I trust in God to guide my way.
I follow Him. He's always there."
But things have changed it seems today.

It's not as popular to do.
To take a stand. To follow Him.
To trust His Word, believe it's true.
It's easier to follow them,

The ones who say, "There is no God,"
Who only trust in what they see.
Say "Those with faith are strange or odd.
The only one to please is me."

I pray dear Lord for those who soar,
Who dare to trust in You once more.

APRIL 28, EMBRACE TODAY

It's fine to have some goals in mind,
To look beyond the daily grind,
About what life might be someday,
But never overlook today.

What's in our future we don't know,
Unlike a movie or a show,
Fast forwarding to have a look,
Or skipping chapters in a book.

Sometimes it's hard to be content.
It's difficult, but here's a hint.
Find cherished moments all around,
Those blessings we've already found.

Embrace each day as though the last
Tomorrow it will be the past.

APRIL 29, STORMS

I thank You Lord through stormy nights,
You lift my faith to scale new heights.

I see the lightning, feel the roar,
Lord give me faith, to dare to soar.

I see Your mighty power displayed.
Your strength, oh Lord, will never fade.

The storms must come, blow through my life,
Some cause me pain, pierce like a knife.

Sometimes a loss brings tears and grief,
Lost in an instant like a thief.

Storms draw me close, I trust in You
To give me strength, my faith renew.

Lord help me fly on eagle's wings,
And share the joy that my heart sings.

I pray that others know Your love,
When storms are raging up above.

APRIL 30, AGING

I'm not quite sure when I grew old.
My body's now a bit more frail.
I bundle more against the cold.
A brisk north wind feels like a gale.

It doesn't seem that long ago
That I could run a faster pace.
But now I walk, my stride is slow,
A jogging trail is not my place.

So far it seems my mind's still strong.
Although my mem'ry tends to fade,
It's good enough to get along.
It still could earn a passing grade.

I pray each day I'm aging well,
So many stories left to tell.

MAY 1, MORNING ROUTINE

I awake every morning, get out of my bed,
Sip on my coffee, clear fog from my head.
I continue to read and to write and to pray,
New insights to see and to capture each day.

I'll admit it's a habit, my daily routine.
Perhaps it's rut but it's polished and clean.
I could call it discipline, that's overdone,
It gives me great pleasure, let's just call it fun.

It's hard to believe it's been over three years
Since I started to capture my hopes and my fears,
To write down in rhyme what I find in my soul.
In my heart I'm still young but the mirror says old.

Now you know how each morning I'm spending my time,
Reading and sipping and spinning a rhyme.

MAY 2, WORDS SPOKEN SOFTLY

It's not my place to just spew words,
But rather touch what's deep inside,
Reach other hearts when they are heard,
Pray sensitivity's my guide.

If words I used were rough and crude,
I doubt they'd make it past the ear.
I see no reason to be rude.
Words kindly spoken, those we hear.

I pray that I treat others well,
That I choose wisely words I say,
And stories that I choose to tell
Will lift a heart and soul today.

Words spoken softly, gentle, kind,
Are words I seek and pray I find.

MAY 3, FINDING GOLD

If I'm too focused on profound,
I'll miss the wondrous all around.
While searching for the next big thing,
I might walk past a golden ring.

Not everything that's glowing, bright
Will give our hearts and souls delight.
Don't miss the small, sometimes it's grand.
Take time to notice, understand.

Sometimes what first looks simple, plain,
We later find is not mundane.
It takes a wise discerning heart
To know the difference from the start.

I pray I let my heart and soul
Determine what to me is gold.

MAY 4, WORDS OF HOPE

May words that I write offer courage and hope,
Help others seek wisdom, the patience to cope.
May the words that I share convey truth that is real
From deep in my soul what I know, what I feel.

May my words speak of treasure beyond earthly realms
With words spoken gently that don't overwhelm,
Provide words of comfort to those in distress,
Show others the pathway to healing and rest.

I pray that my words help show others the way,
So many competing to lead them astray.
It's really quite simple, I don't understand,
Why we resist what God's already planned.

His Son gave His life so that others may live.
There's nothing more precious that He had to give.

MAY 5, LOVE
I Cor 13:4-7

Love is patient, love is kind,
No jealousy, not prone to boast,
No haughty pride or rudeness will you find.
"Seek my own way" is not what's valued most.

Irritation's not the way that love is shown.
Love's memory will not record the wrongs.
Injustices love never will condone,
Finds joy when truth's on top where it belongs.

Love finds hope and will endure,
No giving up, it's not love's way,
A faith in God that is secure
Throughout the storms when skies are gray.

I pray that love inside may grow.
Lord help me learn to let it show.

MAY 6, SIMPLE AND PLAIN

My words are quite simple, they're clear and yet plain.
To me it's the rhythm that drives each refrain.
I try not to clutter the thoughts that I share
With words picked at random to try to add flair.

If the words flow together and sound like a song,
If they're pleasantly soothing and not like a gong,
They'll more likely be heard and then linger a while.
Some songs bring a tear, some a sigh or a smile.

I love to stitch thoughts around one central theme,
Perhaps, just for taste, spoon a bit of whipped cream.
"What's the theme of this ramble?" I'm sure you will ask.
It's a rhyme about rhyming and rhythm - the task.

I try to mix rhythm with simple and plain,
Unscramble the thoughts intertwined in my brain.

MAY 7, REST AND FOLLOW

My life's slowed down, less need to rush.
I now enjoy a slower pace.
I seek God's peace amidst the hush.
I know God's love, His joy, His grace.

So many truths I've yet to learn,
So much that I have yet to know,
Lord grant me wisdom to discern,
Digest the truth that I may grow.

Then help me Lord know how to share,
Find places Lord to read a rhyme.
I don't know how or when or where,
You've made the plans, the place and time.

I trust you Lord to lead the way,
Direct me Lord, you know the day.

MAY 8, MOTHERLY LOVE

There's nothing as soothing as motherly love,
Like a beautiful sunrise, the call of a dove,
Parched fields bathed in rain on a warm summer's eve.
There's nothing so lovely we'll ever receive.

It's a valuable gift that is given each day,
The love of a mother, her own special way.
Like a cavern whose depths we can never explore,
The love of a mother runs deep in her core.

What a blessing to honor them, grateful for life,
To make their day special with freedom from strife,
Perhaps give them flowers, a gift, one or two,
Acknowledging gratitude, love that is true.

The love of my mother in every life phase
Will always be honored for all of my days.
I'm older in age and my mother's now free
To walk golden streets that I too will soon see.

MAY 9, A LONGING

There's a longing inside me that's hard to explain,
That keeps seeking to soar, fly above the mundane.
As I'm searching for words to express what's inside,
I keep flushing out feelings still trying to hide.

Can I journey beyond what is just in my mind?
If I try to probe further, then what might I find?
How far should I reach when I probe in my soul?
I know there's no treasure like silver or gold.

Why am I searching and digging so deep?
Perhaps share with others what's not mine to keep.
God said in His image we're formed, and we're made.
God left us His imprint; I pray it won't fade.

One truth I've discovered by searching inside,
There's a place that's reserved where God's Spirit abides.

MAY 10, MORNING PRAYERS

It's dark outside, the sun's not up.
The house is quiet when I rise.
The coffee maker brews a cup
To help me open up my eyes.

I sit and sip, it's how I start,
A quiet time to read and pray,
A time to stir my sleeping heart.
I pray for words to share today.

I pray for those who mourn inside.
I pray for those enduring pain,
For those whose life's a bumpy ride,
Who've lost a spouse, adjust, remain.

Perhaps for you I lift a prayer,
And others too, though unaware.

MAY 11, A SMILE AND A HOWDY

A smile or a howdy won't likely offend.
They both cost me nothing. I give them for free.
Perhaps I will find that I make a new friend.
Sometimes they just pass and pretend they don't see.

Someone who's hurting may need a good smile.
Perhaps someone's lonely who needs a kind word,
Needs someone to talk to it's been quite a while,
Needs someone to listen, and know they've been heard.

If you're hurting or lonely there's someone who cares.
His love's everlasting. He keeps every tear.
He's ready to listen. He hears every prayer.
He offers you peace. He will drive away fear.

Don't count on a person to meet every need.
Reach out to the Lord and then follow. He'll lead.

MAY 12, LOSS OF A FRIEND

Our friend's now with the Lord above
Surrounded by His perfect love,
Immersed, embraced by perfect peace,
At home at last, all sorrows cease.

Lord help us now, those who remain,
We need Your love to ease the pain.
We're thankful Lord he's now with You,
But still each day we'll miss him too.

We'll miss that ever present smile
But only for a little while.
We know that soon we'll reunite.
We too will know God's perfect light.

We'll have eternity to spend
With those we love and call our friend.

MAY 13, HEALING TOUCH

I lift my friends to God in prayer.
For those in need, to God I pray.
Lord mend those hearts in need of care.
Help them embrace Your love today.

For those who need Your healing touch
I ask You Lord, Your will be done.
You loved each one of us so much,
You came to earth, God's only son.

These earthly bodies do face death
But Lord I ask that You would heal.
You give us Lord our every breath
You died. You rose. Your love is real.

Lord those in pain I know as friends
I pray You'll touch, that they may mend.

MAY 14, WHERE TO SHARE

I pray the Lord leads me to places to share,
Leads me to people who need words of hope.
I need the Lord's guidance. I need to know where
To spread words that share God and help others to cope.

Lord I need Your direction, please show me the way,
The pathway to sharing the words from my heart.
It's the third anniversary of writing most days.
Lord give me the wisdom, to know where to start.

Are there places and people you want me to see?
How do I find them and how do we meet?
Lord You are the focus it's not about me.
Help me follow the footprints You formed with Your feet.

What more shall I do with the thousands of words?
Are there more ways to share them so others have heard?

MAY 15, SHARED FAITH

Should someone ask what I believe,
Can I explain in simple words,
Make clear the faith that I've received,
Deliver well, so I'll be heard?

The words best used are simple, kind.
Shared from the heart and soul inside,
Not empty words that feed the mind.
Just share in love how Jesus died.

He bled and suffered on the cross.
He took my place, he paid the price.
For me to live, He suffered loss.
God sent His Son, my sacrifice.

We all know well that we have sinned.
But God is perfect, just, and true.
Our impure hearts can't enter in.
God made a way for me, for you.

Believe His Son who took our place.
Our sins had sentenced us to die.
Through Him our sin is now erased.
Forever live with God on high.

MAY 16, STILLNESS

In quite stillness solitude
Helps soothe the soul, less prone to brood,
Find peace and calm, much needed rest.
The rhythm slows inside your chest.

Take time to feel the air you breathe,
The healing oxygen receive.
Let go, exhale your cares away
Your mind relaxed above the fray.

Your eyes now close, your soul now free
To search your heart for what to see.
Allow yourself to just abide.
Let all the tension drain, subside.

I pray you find that lasting peace
That will endure and never cease.

MAY 17, STILL HERE

If I were struck by ALS
How would I cope once it progressed
How would I share help others see
I'm still alive I still am me

Inside the shell trapped by disease
Control is gone the muscles freeze
No way to sing or shout or scream
Still more alert than it might seem

With all the love that's trapped inside
No way to let that love outside
I long to speak my thoughts and share
The silence is so hard to bear

Frustration starts to take its toll
As through the years I've lost control
So much to say no way to tell
The ones I love and know so well

I'm still alive alert inside
Within my heart God still abides

MAY 18, THE SONG

As I come before God, and I lift up my prayer,
I am joining with the others as part of a song.
My words a small part, yet He's fully aware
Of each word of the prayer that is centuries long.

Each day we His people lift prayers to the Lord
As we join in the stream of words ancient and old,
Conversations with God whom we love and adore,
A message unbroken that never grows cold.

I consider the saints who are part of that stream,
The prayers they have lifted in days long ago.
I give thanks for each one that the Lord has redeemed.
The number of prayers I'm sure only God knows.

The prayers that we're lifting each day from the heart
Become part of a song and we each sing a part.

MAY 19, FINAL PHASE

A pleasant morning void of rain
A gentle breeze upon my face
As soothing words flow through my brain
Content to live a slower pace

For decades worked in overdrive
Create new paths, new goals achieve
The bleeding edge was where I thrived
To bring to life what we conceived

I now live life in lower gear
I'm cherishing this final phase
It's not a time of life to fear
Instead embrace these final days

Enjoy the pause, life's still worthwhile,
The little things can bring a smile

MAY 20, POETRY

Some things I read quickly, absorb what I've read,
While others I ponder, prefer nice and slow,
Let images linger a while in my head.
Given time they will rise as the yeast inside dough.

Reading lines of a poem I know where to pause,
Each line that I read, a beginning and end.
Some poems seem restless and follow no laws,
While others, like lyrics, words woven to blend.

No matter the form or the texture or style,
A poem's not meant to just skim and read fast.
Like soup it improves if it simmers a while.
Some poems we savor, they linger and last.

Old hymns provide verses I keep in my heart.
Their message brings joy that will never depart.

MAY 21, THE JOURNEY

No matter the journey, how long is the road,
There's rest when it's finished, someday at the end.
The Lord's always with me to lighten my load.
Each day's an adventure. What's 'round the next bend?

I can't see the future or what it will bring,
A mixture of sunshine and thunder and rain.
Lord grant me the courage in hard times to sing.
You pen every verse of my life, each refrain.

Lord give me direction to follow Your lead,
Keep my focus on others and what I can do,
How I can help to reach others in need.
Lord mold me and shape me to be more like You.

One day when my journey through this life's complete,
I'll be in Your presence, bow down at Your feet.

MAY 22, A CANDLE

We're made to be candles, we're made to spread light.
Sometimes it is painful, the wax needs to burn,
But the glow of a candle, a beautiful sight,
Sheds light in the darkness around every turn.

What good is a candle that's never been lit?
Perhaps it's ornate and has beauty and form.
But should it be placed on a shelf to just sit,
Not even shed light when it's dark in a storm?

I know every candle, no matter how small,
Can push back the darkness if given the chance.
I pray that your candle will answer the call.
Let God light your candle and see the flame dance.

As you take time to listen, to pause, and to pray,
May your light shine for others to show them the way.

MAY 23, SET FREE

Do those I know consider me as kind?
Do words I use inspire and offer hope?
What are the faults not seen by me, I'm blind?
Would I be judged a wise man or a dope?

Sometimes it's hard to know how others feel,
How much they trust the words I choose to share.
I pray I'm always genuine and real,
That others plainly see I truly care.

The more that I dig deep, the more I write,
The more I get in touch with what's inside,
Pull back the curtains, fill the rooms with light,
Let others in, find nothing left to hide,

I realize it's not what others see.
It's only by God's grace that I'm set free.

MAY 24, WHY

A pride builds inside during good times in life.
We love to take credit for things that we've done.
But who do we blame when we run into strife,
When the storms in our life seem to block out the sun?

It's sad that so many say, "There is no God,"
Make a fist in defiance and reach toward the sky,
Use evil as proof He's a myth or a fraud.
If God's really there, then demand to know why.

The Lord God is sovereign, His ways beyond mine.
They're not mine to question but rather endure.
He loves me in good times when everything's fine,
But also, through bad times His love is still pure.

Lord I'm humbled and grateful, amazed by Your grace.
You walk with me daily. I feel Your embrace.

MAY 25, HOME

I never thought about it much when growing up,
What kind of person I'd turn out to be.
A small-town boy who loved to play much like a pup.
Those carefree days and friends, still part of me.

A black top road, a front porch swing, my childhood home
Seem distant now but linger still inside.
I traveled 'round the world I've had a chance to roam.
Learned home is more than just where I reside.

Those small-town roots inside will always be a part.
They'll always put a smile upon my face.
A home is built with memories that fill my heart,
A love that binds the heart, not just a place.

I'm grateful Lord for love that formed my cornerstone.
Your love is in my heart. I'll never be alone.

MAY 26, SIMPLE ROOTS

I'm blessed with simple small-town roots
Where folks dressed up in jeans and boots.
No need back then for key or lock,
No need to rush, or check the clock,

Not too concerned with fame or wealth,
Just gratitude for food and health.
The days back then have changed somehow.
Those days gone by seem distant now.

Those roots ran deep and helped me grow.
Those memories from long ago
Still firmly lodged inside my heart,
Forever there, and won't depart,

That firm foundation based on love
From parents, friends, and God above.

MAY 27, HIGHER GOALS

Don't focus on just what not how.
Set higher goals than "Get it done."
Take time to look beyond the now.
What good is wealth if loved by none?

Consider how we live each day.
Make sure our actions show respect,
The things we do, the words we say.
Each day take time to pause, reflect.

We only have one life to live.
Our time is short upon this earth.
How well we learn to love and give,
I think would better measure worth.

Lord keep my heart attuned to You,
Reflect Your love in all I do.

MAY 28, A FRIEND

So many sources of despair,
Don't carry more than you can bear.
Surround yourself with words of hope,
Encouragement to help you cope.

I pray you know and trust a friend,
Someone on whom you can depend
To lend assistance to succeed.
Reach out for help when you're in need.

You too can be a trusted friend
To those in pain who need to mend,
If you're available to share,
Reach out in love to show you care.

Sometimes the hurt is deep inside,
Concealed and covered up with pride.
Sometimes it's hard, but wait and pray,
And God will lead, He'll show the way.

MAY 29, A SUNNY DAY

A pleasant walk, a gentle breeze
A mockingbird with songs to please
Allows my heart and soul to ease
Breathe deep let troubles fade away

The morning sky with puffs of white
The morning sun gives off its light
The flowers bloom with sheer delight
The summer warmth is here to stay

Cold winter days I seldom miss
The spring and fall to me are bliss
Cool mornings rise to top my list
And near the bottom skies of gray

I'm grateful for a sunny day
Still in my heart a child at play

MAY 30, MEMORIAL DAY TRIBUTE

We pause to give honor, lay wreaths at their grave,
Those with the courage, the strong and the brave,
To those who fought valiantly, they paid the price,
Our heads bowed in silence for their sacrifice.

We remember this day those who fought by their side,
Who pause to pay tribute to buddies who've died.
We honor those veterans those who have served.
To them we give thanks, the respect they deserve.

We pray for the loved ones that they left behind.
We pray they know peace and that comfort they find.
Down through generations let's never lose sight
Of the ones who stood bravely defending what's right.

Let's remember each day of this life that we live,
It's not what we gain, rather what we can give.

MAY 31, FAREWELL

Another year comes to an end,
A time of fellowship with friends,
A time to share, discuss, and pray.
Dismissed for summer break to play,

We'll meet again, come back this fall.
We'll have more stories to recall.
The Lord may call a few more home,
Through golden streets in heaven roam.

Our time is short to spend on earth.
Our days were numbered from our birth.
We're blessed with days that still remain,
But know, like Paul, "to die is gain."

We'll once again be gathered here,
Share fellowship and spread some cheer.
I bid farewell until next time,
If I still write, I'll share some rhyme.

JUNE 1, NOTHING NEW

What can I write that's not already penned?
What words will share truth on which others depend?
I just share what I know to be true in my heart,
Words from the Lord that will never depart.

There's nothing I share that is new or unique.
I share what I find, it's God's treasure I seek.
More precious than diamonds, than silver or gold
Are treasures in heaven that never grow old.

I pray that by capturing verses in rhyme,
As a way of conveying the thoughts I opine,
The words provide comfort and soundness of sleep,
Share nuggets of truth that are worthy to keep.

I pray they're consistent with those from God's Word,
Words shared through the ages; I pray they are heard.

JUNE 2, HEART WOUNDS

The days turn gray, skies fill with rain
Accentuating souls in pain.
We mourn the innocent who die,
Those left behind still asking why.

Some blame God instead of men
Who scoff at God, embrace their sin.
The broken hearts, how will they mend?
When will the darkness ever end?

God knows our pain, He hears our voice,
Which path we choose, we have a choice:
Let anger dictate how we live,
Or find the peace that God can give.

God's sovereign, yet we can choose.
How both can be we get confused.
When things go wrong is God to blame
As some who raise a fist proclaim?

God's not obliged to tell me why.
I'd love to know, I'll not deny.
I cannot fully understand,
But know each day I'm in His hands.

I trust in God when skies are gray
Not just when sunshine comes my way.
God's love is real, His comfort's strong
When life's a mess, things seem so wrong.

I know that God is on the throne,
He knows our pain and hears our groan.
I pray that hearts one day will mend,
Allow God's peace to reign within.

JUNE 3, FOREVERMORE

To things of earth I loosely hold,
Try not to keep too firm my grip.
I realize as I grow old,
I'll check no bags my final trip.

There's nothing here I'll need to pack.
My journey to forevermore,
That one-way trip, no ticket back,
I can't conceive of what's in store.

Beyond this realm of time and space
I'll have new eyes and clearly see
The One who put the stars in place,
Who formed the earth by His decree.

Lord help me hold things loosely here.
In time they'll fade and disappear.

JUNE 4, THE MASTER'S TOUCH

If I could write a symphony
With words and verse, not notes or scores,
Could I find words unique to me,
Or just repeat what's come before?

Old instruments still live today.
Their beautiful rich mellow sounds
Are at their best when masters play.
In masters' hands their soul is found.

If instruments improve with age,
Yet always need a master's touch.
Can those who write upon the page
Without their Master mellow much?

I pray I age, grow old with grace,
Until I see my Master's face.

JUNE 5, CELEBRATION

We gather to celebrate our dearest friend.
You've touched many lives in your ninety-five years.
You've shared love and kindness, helped others to mend.
You've been there beside them to dry many tears.

We love your sweet spirit, infectious smile.
You reach out to others in your unique way,
You make them feel special and needed, worthwhile.
Your eyes always sparkle like children at play.

We're so blessed by your presence, your love and your care.
We appreciate you and the life that you live.
We're blessed by the love in your heart that you share,
A reflection of Jesus, with all that you give.

On this special day we share love from our heart,
A love through a bond that our Lord can impart.

JUNE 6, ARTISTIC EXPRESSION

We all need a way of expressing ourselves,
Inside us the essence that we'll never quell.
Artistic expression begins in the heart.
Your gifting determines the form of your art.

For some it's through music expressed in a song.
Some find that an orchestra's where they belong.
Others have beautiful voices and sing,
Together in harmony melodies ring.

Sometimes it's a canvas expressing the soul,
Each painting unique yet a part of a whole.
Perhaps it's with wood or with metal or clay,
That an artist reveals what the heart has to say.

Sometimes it takes shape in the form of a word
That touches the heart when it's spoken and heard.

JUNE 7, FRIENDS

I need my friends upon this earth.
They shelter me from scorching sun.
More valuable than gold is worth,
They sit with me when I can't run.

A friendship's roots grow thick and deep,
Tap wisdom deep beneath the ground.
Their loyalty does not come cheap.
In times of need a friend's around.

Those times when life gets hot and dry,
A friend provides much needed shade.
When life's unfair, I'm asking why,
It's then I cherish friends I've made.

Keep friendships fresh and make some new.
Spend time with friends and be one too.

JUNE 8, THE DOVE

A dove stopped by to say hello,
Just taking in the morning glow,
Soon spread its wings and flew away,
No parting words, goodbyes to say,

Perhaps to find a long-lost mate,
Who long ago found heaven's gate.
I've often heard doves mate for life,
So many seasons, husband, wife.

Throughout the days and nights they share,
They form a long and lasting pair.
Expressing love they sing their song.
They know together they belong.

Somewhere afar I hear its coo,
Somewhere up there where skies are blue.

JUNE 9, IN MY COCOON

An evening 'round the campfire on a clear and starry night
The crackles of the burning wood the distant crickets' song
Reflections from the years gone by
   when everything seemed right
Without the constant stream of news
   portraying worldly wrongs

Sometimes I need to get away and let my soul find peace
I still can travel in my mind to some far distant beach
A gentle stroll beside the lake the distant call of geese
No commentator's diatribe with yet another speech

Sometimes when I need solitude, I spin a small cocoon
I tease my mind and build a scene from places I know well
Perhaps to start a gentle breeze then add a distant loon
Then more detail with colors, sounds,
   perhaps a taste or smell

It's not as good as being there but helps my soul find rest
Perhaps one day I'll go again on yet another quest

JUNE 10, THE MAGNOLIA

The morning brought a cardinal,
   his coat a shiny red.
I briefly glimpsed the reddish brown;
   his darting mate flew by.
He stared at me atop the fence,
   but not a word he said.
Then off he went, his wings spread wide,
   adventures in the sky.

Then a visit from a jay
   just hopping on the fence.
He too was dressed; he wore a suit
   with silver stripes on blue.
He disappeared into the tree.
   I haven't seen him since.
Perhaps he's resting on a nest,
   I haven't seen a clue.

The small magnolia by the fence
   we planted years ago
Is full and thick with foliage now,
   inside it's hard to see.
Each year we watched it fill with bloom,
   put on new leaves and grow.
I think to birds who call it home,
   it's now a family tree.

Now tall, mature, so green and wide,
   majestic it's become.
Extended branches welcoming,
   providing home for some.

JUNE 11, LAUGHTER

Some days it's essential, a good hearty laugh.
When life gets too serious, double the need,
Especially laughter that's on my behalf.
To laugh at myself is essential indeed.

Life's full of humor, it's easy to see.
If I just look around me it's not hard to find.
So why is it harder to laugh about me?
Would it shatter some image I've built in my mind?

I'm not always perfect, of that I am sure.
Plenty of things in my life go awry.
A good dose of laughter's an excellent cure,
If I'm open, I'll find it, I don't have to try.

We all need some laughter, a little each day,
To lighten the troubles that life brings our way.

JUNE 12, A TIME TO REFLECT

I need time every day to relax and reflect,
To search in my heart where my spirit resides.
I cherish that time, I don't often neglect,
Shine light in the crevices, let nothing hide.

It's easy to let all the other stuff fill
All my time and neglect to be still and to pray.
But I lose my direction not knowing God's will.
I need Him to guide me and show me the way.

For me it's a pleasure to capture in rhyme,
To write down the thoughts as they come to my mind,
A way to remember each morning, each time
That I spend with the Lord and the words that I find.

It's a blessing to share them, to let others see,
To take a few moments to set the words free.

JUNE 13, A BETTER PLACE

To make the world a better place
My poetry won't win the race.
I may not know just how or why,
But every day I still can try.

Sometimes the little seeds I plant
Refuse to whither, say "I can't."
The words that enter through the ear
Take root in hearts that yearn to hear.

Some souls have soil that's fertile ground.
They hear the words, find sweet the sound.
I pray the words will linger, stay,
Help those still searching find their way.

I pray each day to God above
He shows me ways to share His love.

JUNE 14, FOR MY WIFE

I pray that healing peace be found
I pray her health would turn around
I pray the grip of pain would leave
Restore her joy, no longer grieve

Lord heal her body, soul, and mind
May all her troubles stay behind
Lord help her sleep, provide her rest
Help her each day know she is blessed

Lord give her strength and faith each day
To face what troubles come her way
Lord help her know and feel Your love
Descend on her, soothe like a dove

Lord hold her close in loving arms
And keep her safe and free from harm

JUNE 15, BITTER WORDS

The words that you speak in the morning in haste
You may eat for dinner, a quite bitter taste.
It's better each morning to hold them and wait
Than find them that evening served up on a plate.

Find words that speak kindly what you have to say.
Provide others comfort to brighten their day.
Life brings enough sorrow, why add to the pile,
When words of encouragement help others smile?

I'm grateful for others with kindness to share,
Who know what to say when life doesn't seem fair,
Who give me perspective from their point of view,
Help me pause and reflect, let my spirit renew.

I pray that I also can do as I write,
Reach out to others, spread wisdom and light.

JUNE 16, DAWN

I love the dawn, grey turns to blue
Those streaks of color, every hue
That time of peace to start my day
In solitude, a time to pray

That time of day I savor most
It's not yet warm, don't think I'll roast
The summer heat, the clear blue skies
The temperature begins to rise

The patio, the morning breeze
Now gently stirring through the trees
Soft words and thoughts flow through my mind
I'll capture them, the ones I find

Jot down my thoughts in words of rhyme
To start my day with quiet time

JUNE 17, FINDING COURAGE

Dark shadows and memories, buried and deep
Can rise up to taunt us in dreams as we sleep.
Holding on to the past can affect how we live.
Find enough courage, let go and forgive.

We cannot undo the mistakes of the past,
So, focus instead on the things that will last.
Plant seeds in the present, perhaps they will grow
Harvests of blessings that others will sow.

Live in the present and what it can be.
A focus on others can help set us free.
Our troubles diminish as we look around.
What once seemed a mountain can shrink to a mound.

There's no need to carry the mem'ries of pain
I pray you find peace as you hear each refrain.
I pray that you're able to find perfect peace,
Find rest in God's hands as your cares are released.

JUNE 18, SAVOR EACH MOMENT

Life's ever changing, each day's a new page,
Those gradual changes that come as we age.
We slowly transition, begin a new phase
That's measured in years or in decades, not days.

One thing that I've learned that for me is now clear;
Don't cling to the past, it's the present that's dear.
Savor each moment as though it's my last.
Don't dwell on the things I can't change in the past.

I'm grateful for memories new ones and old,
But embrace each new day as I see it unfold.
'Til the Lord calls me home, each new day that I live,
I pray that I learn and find new ways to give.

I've been blessed to bless others. I share what I find,
Little bits of myself that I'm leaving behind.

JUNE 19, LAST DAYS OF SPRING

The last remaining days of spring
Cool mornings wain but still I cling
I hold them close and keep them near
Soon say goodbye, come back next year

In summer days with scarce a breeze
I'll find a shade beneath the trees
To watch the squirrels and rabbits play
When summer's heat is here to stay

As I watch spring fade into past
Sometimes reflect "Is it the last?"
And if I knew, what would I change?
Do I have things to rearrange?

Lord help me cherish each new day,
And fill my heart with words to say.

JUNE 20, TROUBLES COME

A dose of troubles every day,
It seems that life is made that way.
Sometimes they linger, want to stay.
I lift them up to God in prayer.

I go through life, live each refrain.
Some days bring sun and others rain,
Including days that come with pain,
If not my own, those close I share.

You bring me calm in stormy seas.
When I am bound, You set me free,
Inside the darkness help me see.
When I'm in need, You're always there.

You bring me peace when life's not fair.
You love me Lord, I know Your care.

JUNE 21, SHADOWS OF THE PAST

Turn around, turn around, have a look, and take heed.
Sift through the ashes, those days of the past.
Hold on to treasures that one day you'll need.
The substance is gone but the memories last.

The things that I do with my life every day,
The plans that I make and the hours that I spend,
The people I meet on the path 'long the way,
May turn into treasure, become a new friend.

The present and future are subject to change.
The days of the past provide context and form.
The shadows they cast may at times appear strange,
Whether blue skies and sunshine or those that bring storms.

Each day in our album we add a new page.
We value our memories more as we age.

JUNE 22, FOR YOU

Each rhyme that I pen is a gift I create
To be opened by others to read and relate.
I pray they are soothing, a comforting balm,
That penetrates deep, to the soul it brings calm.

I pray as I write that my words are sincere,
What I share's from the heart, not just pleasing to hear.
Sometimes it's not easy to share what I feel,
But pray that my words provide courage to heal.

Life is not easy but something we share.
Our load is made lighter by others who care.
I pray you find blessings poured out from above,
Give thanks every morning to God for His love.

I've no way of knowing what you're going through,
Perhaps what I've written was meant just for you.

JUNE 23, OLD FASHIONED RHYME

Poetic verse now blurs a bit I hear.
Sometimes it's hard to find a verse at all,
A different shape from rhymes of yesteryear
Unlike the ones from youth I still recall.

Although quite different what others now do,
Forms others avoid feeling stifled, constrained,
I still prefer old ways, those trusted and true.
How verses and words form inside my brain.

Perhaps it's me who must apologize.
My verses metered, filling lines with rhyme,
Time passed me by I did not realize
Are from another era, place, and time.

For me with rhyme and rhythm still to bloom,
Although old fashioned, still my words can bring,
That I'm allowed, there's still sufficient room
The melodies my heart still longs to sing.

No matter how we form the words we share,
Words still convey with all our heart we care.

JUNE 24, ONE LIFE

We're each given but one life to live,
To learn how to love and to give,
To discover the treasures inside,
And find ways to share and not hide.

"It's better to give than receive,"
Is a concept that's hard to believe.
We're each given gifts to impart.
The best gifts are shared from the heart.

We each need a passion, a drive
To keep us alert and alive.
Don't dwell on regrets when you're old.
Build mem'ries more precious than gold.

I pray that God shows me the way,
To share love with others each day.

JUNE 25, FAITH TO PRAY

I had no intention of writing today.
What else could I possibly have left to say?
Perhaps someone else is in need of a word,
Something to ponder that they've never heard,

Perhaps an old wound that's unwilling to mend,
Or someone who's lonely in need of a friend.
I don't know your name but I'm praying for you.
I pray you find peace and encouragement too.

I'm not there beside you, I can't hold your hand.
There's much about prayer that I don't understand,
But I do have the faith that God hears what we say,
If we speak from the heart and we earnestly pray.

You'll know in your heart if these words are for you.
Down deep in your soul you will know they are true.

JUNE 26, WORDS ON A PAGE

I'm not a prophet nor a sage.
I write my words upon the page,
Arrange the words inside a frame,
Shared from the heart from whence they came.

Is poetry considered art,
Impressions captured from the heart,
Revealing what's inside of me,
My thoughts in words to be set free?

I'm not sure why I choose to share.
How far their reach I'm unaware.
I pen the words and also pray
For those who read these words someday.

I pray you know God's perfect peace.
His blessings daily never cease.

JUNE 27, A WELL-WATERED GARDEN

A garden well-watered, a beautiful sight,
To those who behold it a constant delight.
With roots that are nourished, and leaves bathed with sun
The flowers give pleasure to most everyone.

A beautiful garden first forms in the mind,
Then it takes shape and becomes a design.
Every garden's unique and it changes with age.
There's a beauty in gardens no matter the stage.

May the water of life find its way to your soul.
May its nourishment penetrate, fill every hole.
May the seeds now inside you sprout flowers galore.
May your life be a fragrance that others adore.

Feed your soul daily, let words touch your heart.
Fill it with love and to others impart
The beauty inside you that others may know
The source of the water for gardens to grow.

JUNE 28, PRIDE

When I get in a hurry, life's moving too fast,
I miss all the roses I may have just passed.
The faster I run and the harder I try,
The more my perspective gets skewed, goes awry.

If I'm humble and honest I have to admit,
When I'm running alone, I'm not moving one bit.
When I seek the Lord's help and I take time to pray,
He gives me direction and shows me the way.

Why do I wait to admit when I'm wrong?
Why do I keep running solo so long?
The hurdles are higher. I'm losing my stride.
At the end of the day, it is usually pride.

"I'm in need of Your help," is my one simple prayer.
Lord I'm grateful You give me Your love and Your care.

JUNE 29, OPEN JOURNAL

Why do I write? Are my motives not pure?
Is it wrong to pen words that perhaps will endure?
Should I try to find words to express what's inside?
Should I share them with others and not let them hide?

I find pleasure in melodies, rhythm, and rhyme.
I don't think it's frivolous, wasting my time.
It helps me to capture and form in my mind
The thoughts that emerge from inside that I find.

I try to relate what's inside that I feel,
Find words to express what for me I find real.
It's more of a journal that's mainly for me,
But I don't keep it sealed with a lock and a key.

If anyone's interested, they can come read,
Perhaps if I share, I'll touch someone in need.

JUNE 30, HONEST AND PLAIN

My poetry's simple, just honest and plain,
You won't find them haughty, pretentious or vain.
They tend to be lyrical, pleasing to hear,
But also, straight forward, transparent, and clear.

If I share from the heart and reveal what's inside
It begins to get easier, nothing to hide.
It's the same when I come to the Lord and I pray,
He wants me to share what my heart has to say.

I humble myself and I pray from my heart.
He already knows me, he knows every part.
We've shared life together, I'm blessed He's my friend,
But also, my savior when this journey ends.

My soul and my spirit will rise and be free.
I'll be in His presence. He's waiting for me.

JULY 1, TRUST GOD

Why nations blessed by God above
Who proudly state, "In God we trust,"
Would turn away, reject His love,
And follow those who turn to dust,

Is hard for me to comprehend.
Why choose to follow those who say,
"There is no God. I am your friend.
Just follow me, I'll lead the way."

There is a God who's in control.
His love is pure, His justice true.
I give to Him my heart and soul,
I pray that you will trust Him too.

It's not too late to take a stand,
Turn back to God, He'll bless our land.

JULY 2, TURBULENCE

When life hits some turbulence none could have guessed,
I have to dig deep so I don't get depressed.
I have to keep reading and praying each day,
Seek the Lord's guidance to show me the way.

Each night in my bed as I drift off to sleep,
I count all my blessings instead of just sheep.
As I number the ways that I've truly been blessed,
I find comfort and peace and my body can rest.

I envision the times in the past and recall
How the Lord picked me up after stumbles or falls.
He helps me through troubles, He hears every prayer.
His love's unconditional. He's always there.

In the midst of the hard times, I know in my heart
The Lord walks beside me, He'll never depart.

JULY 3, GOD'S PEACE

A quiet peace begins inside,
Not something forced upon my mind,
A peace that only God provides.
I trust the Lord, His peace I find.

Where peace begins to touch my thoughts
Is in my heart not in my brain.
A battleground where foes are fought
For peace that overcomes the pain.

The war's been won I know His peace,
A peace that's built on solid rock.
It's strong and firm, will never cease.
I pray that those who doubt or mock,

Who Find no peace inside their soul
Allow the Lord to make them whole.

JULY 4, FREEDOM

As we celebrate freedom, the stripes and the stars,
Remember our history, we've made it so far.
Remember the country and people we are.
Our country's much more than we see on the news.

I'm weary of rhetoric, constant debate,
Those stirring up trouble and peddling hate.
It's time for a change and I pray we don't wait,
That we all come together, respectfully choose,

Find value in differences, seek compromise.
I pray we find statesmen who'll once more arise,
Speak only truth and not tolerate lies.
It's not just elections to win or to lose.

It's not about buttons and slogans and hats,
It's not lining pockets with bills full of fat,
Rather wisdom and judgment, not straining at gnats.
Find those whose integrity's not just a ruse.

Let's pray for our country, not slumber or snooze,
Pray for God's blessing, pray He'll not refuse.

JULY 5, WORDS TO SHARE

Only the Lord can I turn to and trust.
The things that now glitter will tarnish and rust.
I look to the Lord who is ruler of all.
Take my eyes off of Him, then I stumble and fall.

In this life we face sorrow, some heartache and grief.
Some troubles come suddenly, strike like a thief.
I'm never quite certain what each day will bring,
But I know He is with me, my soul can still sing.

The Lord provides guidance, His words always true.
His love lifts my soul to refresh and renew.
If I take time each morning to read and to pray,
He gives me the strength that I need for the day.

Lord thank You for loving me, hearing my prayer.
Thank You for helping me find words to share.

JULY 6, REFLECTING HIS WORD

Each day as I ponder, I read, and I write,
I pray I'm reflecting God's love and his light.
I pray that the words that I pen, and I share
Help others know Jesus, His love and His care.

I've known Him for decades, He's with me each day.
He leads me and guides me. He shows me the way.
He's always beside me, His love never fails.
I know in the end that His love will prevail.

He offers compassion. He knows every need.
His Words provide wisdom if only I'll read.
No longer in bondage my soul is set free.
No longer in darkness my eyes can now see.

The love that He offers is not mine alone.
I pray that you know Him before you're called home.

JULY 7, THE PROCEDURE
(A bit of levity)

Tomorrow's the day, but today is the prep.
It is carefully planned, I must follow each step.
My diet's controlled, I can't eat what I please.
I think I can do it, I hope I don't sneeze.

I tank up on liquid, I force it all down.
It looks like an ocean, I hope I don't drown.
The procedure's tomorrow, the worst is today.
You'd think that by now they'd have found a new way.

I questioned the doc, "Is this something I need?"
He explained it's importance, I finally agreed.
I gave my permission to probe all around.
I hope in the end that our judgment was sound.

As visions of torture play tricks in my head,
The word colonoscopy conjures up dread.

JULY 8, OLD BLOOMS

The verses blur a bit I hear.
It's not like days of yesteryear.
Sometimes no verses form at all,
Unlike the ones that I recall.

Perhaps I must apologize.
It's me who did not realize
My verses metered, filled with rhyme,
Belong another place and time.

I hope there's still sufficient room
For rhyme and rhythm still to bloom.
Although old fashioned, still can bring
A word my heart still longs to sing.

Although it's not what others do,
Won't blaze new trails find something new,
I don't feel stifled or constrained.
It's how words form inside my brain.

I hope the shape and form of words
Will not impact how they are heard,
No matter how we choose to share,
The words convey that we still care.

JULY 9, COMMON GROUND

We all will find places where we disagree.
It is through different lenses we're given to see.
It is through different journeys that we've come to be.
But also, there's harmony, shared common ground.

If we focus on differences closing our minds,
Then we stay in the shadows, grow partially blind.
We miss out on blessings we'd otherwise find.
Life's full of blessings if we look around.

Step out of the shadows embracing God's light.
Life's more about loving than proving we're right.
We all have our differences, background or plight.
Why let them divide us, confuse, and compound?

The Lord sets us free, we are no longer bound.
Lord help us unite, may Your blessings abound.

JULY 10, WHY WRITE?

What happens to words that I write, and I share?
Will anyone read them? Will anyone care?
If I capture the visions I see in my mind,
It helps me see clearly to share what I find.

Should I limit my verses, and carefully choose?
Why should I hold back? I have nothing to lose.
Perhaps there are others who'll hear what I say.
Find those who relate and who feel the same way.

If I write what's inside me and share what I feel,
Will the words that I've written help someone else heal?
Can words from my heart and from deep in my soul
Penetrate others and help them be whole?

I think that's the purpose that drives me to write,
Help someone now hurting in darkness find light.

JULY 11, COMFORTING MEMORIES

I remember the days that I spent on the lake,
Skis gliding on water outside the boat's wake.
It's fun to recall, glad I still can enjoy,
Remembering days that I spent as a boy.

Early mornings of fishing, the water like glass,
I'd cast out a spinner in hopes of a bass.
We'd troll along shorelines with low hanging trees,
The morning so quiet, no hint of a breeze.

In the evening a fish fry with neighbors and friends,
Or a picnic on water to see the day end.
Late in the evening, no light from the sun,
We'd get in the boat, there were trot lines to run.

We're still building memories all through our life.
Those visions bring comfort to ease times of strife.

JULY 12, FAITH TESTED

Sometimes the Lord's ways are a mystery to me,
Reach beyond the horizon my eyes can now see,
Far exceeding the realms that extend beyond time.
Yet His love in my heart can still blossom in rhyme.

Sometimes in life's journey when things go awry,
I find myself asking, "Lord please, tell me why."
But then I remember, just trust and obey,
The Lord gives me strength that I need for today.

My faith, when it's tested, if healthy and strong,
Will carry me through, when the path's dark and long.
One day I will see and at last understand,
How my life had a purpose, fit into a plan.

One thing that I know and of this I am sure,
The Lord's always with me, His love's always pure.

JULY 13, LOVE THRIVES
(To my darling wife)

My dancin' shoes darlin' need polish,
No longer be cuttin' a rug.
I doubt folks would still call me stylish.
Come close 'cause I still love to hug.

You still cause my brown eyes to sparkle.
You still bring a laugh or a smile.
I'm now a bit weathered and wrinkled,
But loving you 's always in style.

We've walked many pathways together.
The good and the bad we've survived.
No matter how stormy the weather,
Our love got us through and still thrives.

We still have some mountains and valleys
To cross before God calls us home.
More flowers in meadows to see,
More pine covered pathways to roam.

I'll always be grateful my darlin', my wife,
That you've been my partner for life.

JULY 14, UNIQUELY DESIGNED

I'm unique and complex, as is all of mankind.
Designed for a purpose to walk on this earth.
There's no other me that I ever will find,
Lord help me discover my talents and worth.

I search for the truth and I share what I find.
Some may agree with the words that I write,
What I hear with my heart and I pen with my mind.
Others stay skeptical, not sure I'm right.

I try to encourage with words that I pen,
With lyrical poetry share from the heart,
Reach deep inside me and share what's within,
Pray others relate to the words I impart.

May the Lord bless and keep you each day of the year.
May His light shine upon you, His Words may you hear.

JULY 15, WEAVING THOUGHTS

I love to weave my thoughts in rhyme,
Perhaps compose a book sometime.

Our books can play a special role
To touch our heart and reach our soul.

When rhymes are fun to hear and say,
Impressions linger, last, and stay.

They find a home inside our brain.
We hear them echo each refrain.

We ponder phrases of each line,
"What other treasures can I find?"

They stir the scenes of long ago,
Attach themselves, we can't let go.

The metered cadence for each word
I pray brings hope as it is heard.

I pray the melody you hear,
Will stir old scenes that you hold dear.

JULY 16, WHAT REMAINS

Sometimes I need to sit and rest.
I may have lost a bit of zest.

I know that I have passed my prime,
Not sure what's left of earthly time.

Perhaps it's just the summer heat.
No need to yield, declare defeat.

It's not yet time to sit and wait,
Regardless of my future fate.

I'll make the best of what remains,
Endure the winds, the storms, the rains.

I'm sure I'll see some sunny days,
Music concerts, local plays.

I plan to write more rhymes to share
With friends who know how much I care.

This body's old, my spirit thrives,
I pray each day my words touch lives.

JULY 17, GENTLE WORDS

I think a kind and gentle word
Is one more likely to be heard.
A peaceful word can soothe the soul.
We need more folks to fill that role.

My soul needs quiet time alone,
Not constant chatter from the phone.
Some time in quiet solitude
Restores my peace and lifts my mood,

A time to rest and just abide,
A time to stop and look inside,
To pause, reflect, and be aware,
Each heartbeat and each breath of air.

When I spend time in quiet prayer,
I find more gentle words to share.

JULY 18, WATER OF LIFE

My spirit needs water from life giving rain.
In the desert a garden is hard to maintain.
Why live in a wasteland all dusty and dry,
When my soul could bloom freely with water nearby?

The life-giving water that flows from a stream
Still waters my garden it's not just a dream.
It waters my soul as I drink from that spring.
My heart is refreshed, I continue to sing.

The source of the water will never run dry.
Eternal refreshment my soul never dies.
It's nothing to hoard rather something to share.
To keep it a secret is simply not fair.

The water is plentiful not just for me.
Don't let your soul wither when it could be free.

JULY 19, REFRESHED

When life appears it might unravel,
Sometimes I take the car and travel,

Park in a shade among the trees,
Get out and walk and feel the breeze.

Stop to hear the woodland sounds.
The birds sing out, squirrels scamper 'round.

Inhale the air, look toward the sky,
I see an eagle, watch him fly.

It clears my head to take a break
Before some task I undertake.

A quiet place to rest and pray,
Give thanks that God's prepared the way.

Refreshed, recharged, my soul at rest,
So many ways I know I'm blessed.

With eagle's wings I long to soar.
Above the trees I see much more.

JULY 20, FINDING WISDOM

The beginning of wisdom is found in God's word,
Then allowing my heart to accept what I've heard.
His words are still true and won't lead me astray,
If I have the faith to just trust and obey.

When I'm headstrong and stubborn and focused on me,
Ignoring God's wisdom, I no longer see.
When I seek the Lord's guidance it's then that I'm wise.
He will answer my plea and He'll open my eyes.

I don't understand why I'm so often prone
To think I'm in charge and can live on my own.
Why resist what is good and will profit my soul,
Go off on a tangent, think I'm in control?

I need the Lord's guidance to live every day.
If I ask, He will hear me and show me the way.

JULY 21, DAYS WITH HAZE

The sun's come up another day.
I long to see the morning light.
The clouds rise up to block each ray.
Diffused the sun is not as bright.

The sky, once blue, now just a haze,
The sun, obscured, no longer glows,
As though it's covered with a glaze,
Infusing rhymes that I compose.

Yet words I write come from the heart,
With rhyme and rhythm show I care.
I pray they'll soothe not tear apart.
I pray it's love that I can share.

I pray the love of God shines through.
I pray this day He blesses you.

JULY 22, NOT JUST FOR ME

I write, I share, but who will read?
I pray my words aren't just for me.
I pray someday they'll meet a need.
Perhaps they'll help set someone free,

Introduce them to God's Word.
If I can share and get it right,
Put down in rhyme what I have heard,
I pray that others seek God's light.

Perhaps they'll search, ask "Is it true?"
Someone enticed to prove me wrong,
Convinced inside the sky's not blue,
I pray God's love becomes their song.

I pray they find God's only Son,
Who paid the price, the work is done.

JULY 23, WORDS FORM INSIDE

The words begin to form inside,
Up from my soul into my mind,
Exposed, no need to crouch and hide,
Set free to let another find.

If they are meant for me alone,
Then why the urge to write and share?
We're more than merely flesh and bone,
Words help us say, "I'm here. I care."

So many folks I'll never meet,
Won't have a chance to sit and talk,
Nor even pass them on the street
Some summer day out for a walk.

I share my heart expressed in word,
Perhaps through rhyme my song is heard.

JULY 24, TREASURE INSIDE

Our bodies are fragile like jars made of clay,
Yet formed as a place where the Lord can reside.
His Spirit's eternal, will never decay.
I'm amazed every morning His treasure's inside.

When days fill with troubles, I'm hurried and rushed,
When life looks perplexing and doesn't seem fair,
I know the Lord's with me my spirit's not crushed.
Though life can be daunting I need not despair.

When life knocks me down, it is hard to find joy
I look to the Lord, He's the one I can trust.
His love is eternal, no one can destroy.
My spirit's with Him though this body's just dust.

God's mysteries are deep, but I know in my heart
He'll always be with me, we're never apart.

JULY 25, TROUBLED DAYS

Some days are dark, the skies are gray.
It seems so hard to maintain hope.
More troubles mount most every day.
Sometimes in life it's hard to cope.

I put my faith in Christ alone.
He gives me life, protects my soul,
I know the Lord's still on the throne.
He'll lead me on, attain life's goal.

I don't know what this day will bring,
What troubles lurk behind the door.
I pray, inside, my heart can sing.
Lord give me wings to fly once more.

Lord light the way through troubled days.
I lift You up. I give You praise.

JULY 26, ANOTHER MRI

Today another MRI,
A noisy beast that's loud and tight.
It helps to spread my wings and fly,
Allow my mind to soar in flight.

They saw a spot. They need to know.
They'll look inside my skull and brain.
If that one spot decides to grow,
The MRI can ascertain.

I have no pain inside my head,
An incidental find last spring.
I don't have any fear or dread.
I pray it's still a little thing.

The neurosurgeon checks the spot,
Determines if it's grown or not.

JULY 27, IN BETWEEN

It's in between heartbeats, the ebb and the flow,
When my heart takes a pause that I'm truly at rest.
In life I need times when I'm not on the go.
It's times when I'm still that are sometimes the best.

As my body grows older that time in between
I cling to more tightly, a much-valued prize.
A time to find treasures that cannot be seen,
To search with my heart and not just with my eyes.

I value some solitude, time to reflect,
Quiet stillness of morning each day to begin.
I find it refreshing and seldom neglect
The silence, the stillness, my trusted old friends.

I jot down my thoughts and I form them to share.
"May they help someone's journey," is always my prayer.

JULY 28, TUNE MY HEART

I rise up early, stretch, and yawn,
As morning light begins to dawn.
A quiet time to pray and write,
Reach out to God to be my light.

Lord tune my heart to hear Your voice.
Lord guide my way, make clear each choice.
I need Your guidance every day.
You light my path, show me the way.

Provide me strength to follow You.
You give me life, Your words are true.
Lord give me words to write Your song
That I may sing the whole day long.

Let others know they too can sing,
Know You as Savior, Lord, and King.

JULY 29, TIME TO PAUSE

Most poems are best when taken slow.
Take time to pause and truly hear.
Let words sink in, have time to grow.
There's likely more that will appear.

A mind can hear as words emerge,
And form a tune inside a head.
A heart absorbs and feels a surge,
Until at last the soul is fed.

Lord help me seek that which is good.
Read what is pure, words that are true,
That help me grow when understood.
Discover truths I never knew.

Lord feed my soul with words of old.
Instill in me a heart of gold.

JULY 30, FRAGILE CONTAINERS

Entrusted to bodies so fragile and weak,
God chose as the place where His Spirit resides.
He has chosen the lowly, the humble, the meek.
There's so little room in a heart full of pride.

We're fragile containers, the treasure's within,
God's light from above that He placed in our heart.
We answered His calling, let new life begin.
Infused with His love we now have a new start.

Our bodies still fragile know sorrow and pain.
The Lord provides comfort and gathers our tears.
He is the source of our strength to regain.
He lights our path; we can walk without fear.

The Lord in His majesty soon will return,
His light and His glory we'll fully discern.

JULY 31, TRANSITIONS

Sometimes transitions can shock to the core.
Suddenly life's not the same anymore.
We like status quo, things to stay as they were.
Sometimes we foresee that a change will occur.

It's hard to face change, not an easy embrace.
Looking back, we remember a time or a place.
Transitions can cause us to stumble or fall,
Or perhaps, if alert, we will hear the Lord's call.

The biggest transition takes place in our heart.
Just trust in the Lord is the best place to start.
Sometimes a decision to leave or to stay
Is more about yielding, "Lord You lead the way.

"I'm ready to listen, to hear, and to heed.
I'm ready to follow wherever You lead."

AUGUST 1, LETTING GO

Lord You're in control, help me know what to say.
Help me learn how to listen to You as I pray.
I'm not in control, help me listen and learn.
In You I have life, it's not something I earn.

If I seek on my own what the outcome should be,
Then I'm walking in darkness, Your light I can't see.
Help me to trust You in all that You do.
Give me the faith to know Your Words are true.

It's not up to me to determine my fate,
But in prayer bring my burdens and then to just wait.
To trust that Your timing is always the best,
Know You'll lead me through it, regardless the test.

Lord help have faith to turn loose and let go,
To put into practice the truths that I know.

AUGUST 2, YOUR LOVE

Your grace is sufficient, Your love is so true.
Life's troubles come frequently, You get me through.
You bring me light, I can more than endure.
You lift me up with Your love that is pure.

Lord thank You for loving me, help me today
To see all the blessings that You send my way.
Lord help mend my wings so again I can soar,
Reach heights even greater than I've known before.

Lord You bring me joy though surrounded by strife,
You lift me up and You fill me with life.
Help me find words to express how I feel.
The love that's inside me from You is so real.

Lord fill me with music that my heart can sing.
Help others to see all the love that You bring.

AUGUST 3, FADED MEMORIES

The mem'ries from childhood may fade but still call.
Those early life glimpses I fondly recall,
A trip to downtown, and a stroll 'round the square.
Folks stopped to say howdy, to tussle my hair.

I'd stop near the corner and watch for a while
The men playing checkers, a joke and a smile.
A barrel of wood held their board as they played
In front of the store 'neath the awning for shade.

I've mem'ries of Mosely's, not there anymore,
Its long counter of marble, the tile on the floor.
I remember the milk shakes and also the floats,
Root beer and ice cream, sometimes cherry coke.

Those days long ago I now cherish like gold,
The fragrance of flowers in pots as we'd stroll,
The smiles and the greetings from those we would see.
Those mem'ries from childhood are still part of me.

Early days in a small town are cherished and dear.
Those images linger with each passing year.

AUGUST 4, STORIES THAT LINGER

You may know I love words that are metered and rhymed,
Even better a story with wisdom entwined,
A story well written that touches the soul,
A story that lingers long after it's told.

Some stories for children read after we're grown
Will offer new insights that we'd never known.
The stories from childhood not read for a while
Can bring back some mem'ries that make our hearts smile.

As parents or grands when we take time to read,
To share with the children, we help them succeed.
Reading a story so others can hear
Is a pastime that's fading with each passing year.

It's a worthwhile endeavor I pray will not end.
To share a good book is to make a new friend.

AUGUST 5, WORD I WRITE

Until the time when words won't form,
My mind has given way to storms,
I'll try to listen every day.
Write words my heart may choose to say.

I write them down and set them free,
Not mine to keep or hoard for me.
I never know what words will come,
How far they'll reach or mean to some.

Not every rhyme is cheerful, glad.
Sometimes my words are born from sad.
The words express the way I feel.
I write them down to help me heal.

I pray the words, the lines I write,
Reflect God's love and shine His light.

AUGUST 6, WORDS BLOOM

To contemplate a brand-new book,
To see the concept bake and cook,
When just a bud, not yet a rose,
Its beauty forms, takes shape, and grows.

It's hard to know just how or when
The seed was planted deep within.
When people ask, "How do I start?"
I say "Express what's in your heart.

"It means reach deep inside of you.
What's there that's meaningful and true,
Uniquely yours that shines like gold?
You'll find your story to be told."

The words will come. You'll set them free.
Your rose will bloom for all to see.

AUGUST 7, MORNING DEW

The year I turned seventy I learned that rhyme
Is a pass time I love, good investment of time.
It helps me to capture the thoughts that pass through.
Sometimes they linger and settle like dew.

I ponder each morning, put thoughts on the page.
I think about life, how it mellows with age.
I journey through mem'ries, those days I was young,
How many more songs I have left to be sung?

I'm grateful for mornings to ponder and write,
When dawn is approaching, it soon will be light.
The morning will break and soon burn off the haze,
It takes a bit longer in life at this phase.

I'm grateful for memories, they still inspire,
Like old friends and laughter, the warmth of a fire.

AUGUST 8, JOYFUL SPIRIT

I bring you a sonnet; I can't end your pain.
I pray as you listen, you let your soul soar.
I pray you find love as you read each refrain.
I pray for a moment the pain you'll ignore.

I wish I could help you to know life pain free,
Remove all the ailments your body has known,
To walk in the sunshine, cause hurting to flee.
I pray your soul's joyful though your body may groan.

I pray that your body will find ways to heal
No longer restrict you and tug at your soul.
I pray you find freedom to match how you feel
To soar as an eagle, new sights to behold.

I pray that the sonnet that I pen with love,
Will help you find peace that God sends from above.

AUGUST 9, LIFT US UP

Lord lift us up on eagles' wings,
Discover joy that we may sing.
Lord give us breath, may we express
With words that others may be blessed.

Your love's beyond this earthly sphere.
One day we'll see, the fog will clear.
We'll fully know and understand
Your perfect will, Your master plan.

Each day with troubles we endure,
You lift us up, Your love is pure.
Your love's beyond this earthly plane,
Extends throughout Your vast domain.

Lord help us daily trust in You.
Our faith is strong. Your words are true.

AUGUST 10, OUR FAITH

I much prefer days blue, not brown.
Sometimes when days just wear me down,
My smile seems painted like a clown.
Lord lift me up, Your plan reveal.

When news of heartache, toil, and strife
Becomes a major part of life,
When healthy days evade my wife,
I pray dear Lord, please help her heal.

Lord give us eyes to see the blue,
Cling to Your love we know is true.
No matter what we're going through,
We follow You, to You we yield.

We live by faith, not how we feel.
Our faith is strong. Your love is real.

AUGUST 11, OLD STYLE

Perhaps it's old fashioned, this writing in rhyme,
This forming of words so they're spoken in time.

I guess the style fits, I'm old fashioned myself.
Not yet in an urn to be placed on a shelf,

I find that my heart still has plenty to say.
I find it's best shared in an old-fashioned way.

Some are put off by the way that I share,
While others ignore me and don't really care.

Though my rhymes are old fashioned each one carries love.
I pray they convey love that comes from above.

Sometimes it's encouragement shared from the heart,
Or even some wisdom that I can impart.

I guess I'll keep writing if only a few
Are touched when the love from my heart can come through.

I pray that the words that I put on the page,
Help others find courage regardless of age.

AUGUST 12, BIRTHDAY GREETINGS

As birthday greetings come my way,
Sent out in love, I read each line.
I'm touched by thoughts that they convey.
I'm blessed with friends, well-aged like wine.

I'm grateful that I have my sight.
My vision now is clear and true.
It's easier for me to write,
Express my gratitude to you.

I'm thankful for the ones who read
The words I write, and post, and share.
I pray perhaps they meet a need,
As I express God's love and care.

I grateful for each birthday wish,
Your words, like cake, are so delish.

AUGUST 13, LIFE'S PATH

Another notch upon life's belt,
They seem so close together now.
Don't know the years that I've been dealt,
Don't know the day, not when or how.

I'll try to live my life today
As though this day ends up my last.
Make sure the words I have to say
Reflect God's love when I have passed.

Passed through the veil, immortal life,
A life without the bounds of time,
Not weighted down by age or strife,
Behold the beauty of sublime.

This earthly life I'm passing through
Is just a path to something new.

AUGUST 14, LET SADNESS GO

Don't hold the sadness, let it go.
Make room to let the blessings flow.
God heals the soul. He can restore
What joys you've lost and so much more.

God's Holy Spirit can reside
Inside the heart and there abide.
Reach out and take the Master's hand,
Accept His love, fulfill His plan.

His love each day will set you free
Restore your sight and let you see
The love and beauty all around,
The majesty yet to be found.

I pray for music in your heart.
May any sadness soon depart.

AUGUST 15, SIGNPOSTS

If I could illuminate scripture each day
And capture the essence of what the words say,
Mix in God's Spirit that lives in my soul,
Perhaps in a small way I'd fulfill a role.

If I mentioned the scriptures that Jesus can heal,
Would it help others know and affect how they feel?
Perhaps if I write of the joy I have found,
Others will find it and spread it around.

I try to share more than a rhyme about trees,
Or a walk in the woods or the birds and the bees.
I try to share wisdom once read from a scroll,
Preserved through the ages more precious than gold.

I pray I paint signposts that help show the way,
Lead others to scriptures to read what they say.

AUGUST 16, TRUST TRUTH

The world may seem a frightful place,
But what have I to fear or dread?
I have a friend who's full of grace.
I choose to trust in Him instead.

He's always there to lift me up.
He comforts me when I am blue.
Inside my heart He fills my cup.
He gives me life. His words are true.

Lord help me hear with all my heart,
Discern the truth inside Your Word,
That's filled with wisdom to impart.
I pray each day that I have heard.

You've placed Your love inside of me.
Lord help me share, let others see.

AUGUST 17, LIFE IS A GIFT

Life is a gift, it's not something to waste,
Yet not to be opened with hurry and haste.
No matter the paper, the wrapping, the cost,
It's what's on the inside that must not be lost.

No matter the color, the shape, or the size,
Each life's to be cherished, a valuable prize.
Each life is unique and we each have a name.
We're each slightly different, yet also the same.

We each form a part of the same human race.
We share the same journey at this time and place.
We're part of this era, this short span of years.
Inside there's a melody others should hear.

Find what's inside you, there's music to share.
Open your heart and show others you care.

AUGUST 18, MAY LOVE SHINE

Who would have thought well past my prime
That I would learn I love to rhyme?
It's like a daily journal now
I'm not quite sure the what or how.

I still have so much more to learn,
So much remains yet to discern.
I love to reach inside my soul.
I never know what will unfold.

If I am brave enough to share,
Reveal to others love and care,
From words that form inside my head,
Perhaps the love I've found can spread.

I pray God's love will shine through me,
Be bright enough that others see.

AUGUST 19, MAJESTIC BEAUTY

I long to soar on eagle's wings
Above the earth, above the trees,
Hear melodies the angels sing,
Glide through the air atop the breeze.

The mountain tops, snow covered peaks,
Majestic beauty 'neath the sky,
They make no sound and yet they speak.
They lift their Maker's name on high.

The waterfalls that feed the streams,
Flow into meadows down below,
Sustaining life, much more it seems
Than simply rain or melted snow.

Each snowflake brings a gift of love,
Floats down to earth from up above.

AUGUST 20, SUBTLE CHANGE

Each day seems much like all the rest.
Today's much like the day before.
Sometimes the days seem like a test.
Some days are hard, more like a chore.

The subtle changes day by day,
Become more visible with years.
Our earthly bodies formed from clay,
Soon fade away and no one hears.

The memories we leave behind,
The cherished moments we thought grand,
Now lost and seldom brought to mind,
Return to earth like grains of sand.

The treasures that I build on earth
Are not the ones of lasting worth.

AUGUST 21, SHARING BOLDLY

How many more lines are still hiding inside?
I search for the words that still lurk in the deep.
I probe in the depths to find where they reside.
Once found I decide on the ones I should keep.

Are they real, did I find them, or did they appear,
Rise up from the shadows still wearing a mask?
Do I risk sharing boldly or hold back in fear?
How much should I share? To decide is my task.

To share from the heart requires courage and love.
Once started it's easier letting folks know.
Sharing light from inside that God sent from above,
I pray others see and are touched by the glow.

I pray for the wisdom to know what to share,
For words to help others find His love and care.

AUGUST 22, SING ALONG

I'd like to pen a lively tune,
A song that anyone can croon,
A song that puts a little pep
Into our walk, our stride, our step.

I love the songs that bring a smile,
That help us laugh just for a while.
I love to see your smiling face.
Just hum along, pick up the pace.

If you can't whistle, hum, or sing,
Then grab a bell and let it ring.
Join in the chorus shout it out,
Sing loud and clear and leave no doubt.

Let's tell the world we have a song.
We're gonna sing it all day long.

AUGUST 23, SHARE WITH A FRIEND

My rhymes capture thoughts that I'd share with a friend.
I search for the words as I share from my heart.
Each has a beginning, a middle, and end.
The challenge is finding a good place to start.

If I try to embellish the words that I write,
Sometimes I get lost and I take the wrong trail.
If I keep my mind focused and never lose sight
Of the reason for sharing then words will prevail.

If my theme is uplifting and words that I pen
Help others find joy and God's peace in their soul,
Then I count it a victory, I call it a win.
If I've helped spread His light, I've accomplished my goal.

I pray you find comfort in words that I share.
Pass them on to another to show love and care.

AUGUST 24, GOD WILL

Someone is hurting and suffers today.
I don't know your name, but this prayer is for you.
It's you I lift up and for you that I pray.
God hears our prayers and I know that it's true.

Perhaps it's an ache that's down deep in your soul,
A fear that has gripped you and hurt your resolve.
Reach out to the Lord, know that He's in control.
No problem's too big that the Lord cannot solve.

Perhaps it's a physical pain that won't cease.
You're weary of hurting and sleep's hard to find.
I pray for your healing, but most of all peace.
May the joy in your heart soothe your body and mind.

I pray that your faith remains healthy and strong.
Know God's in control and will right every wrong.

AUGUST 25, VISION REVIVED

My vision had yellowed and dimmed as I'd aged,
Just gradually changing a little each year.
"Get cataract surgery. You're at that stage."
I mustered the courage to get past the fear.

I recall being told it would help me relax,
Then a voice in distance, "It's time to arise."
The left eye was done, the next week I was back.
It quickly was over, new sight in both eyes.

The sky that was gray is a beautiful blue,
My vision, once blurry, is clear and alive.
The colors, now vivid, take on a new hue,
Elated my vision, once dim, is revived.

I pray that my heart's not diminished in sight.
I pray it sees clearly reflecting God's light.

AUGUST 26, INSIDE A CAVE

Sometimes it seems I'm in a cave.
The air is stale, so little light.
Is this the end? Is this my grave?
When will it end, this darkest night?

I long to laugh at least once more,
Look forward to another day,
Embrace my life like once before,
Fight off the darkness and decay.

What's brought about this dark and doom?
When did I sink into this pit?
I much prefer the light to gloom.
I pray I'll soon be rid of it.

I'll find a way and I'll climb out.
I'll overcome. I have no doubt.

AUGUST 27, POETIC EXPRESSION

So many poems are written today,
Expressions without a particular form.
I love writing verses the old-fashioned way.
I love rhyme and rhythm, for me it's my norm.

I love when they flow with a lyrical sound.
Sometimes I hear music that forms in my head.
The beat of the rhythm keeps swirling around,
To help me remember the words that were said.

Some prefer freedom to write poems in prose,
For others, impressions expressed with free verse.
No matter the form or the method they chose,
We're invited inside; in their thoughts to immerse.

Poetic expression that comes from the soul
Will always be with us; it still has a role.

AUGUST 28, FRIENDSHIPS

I pray I'm never void of friends,
The ones who care through ups and downs,
The ones on whom I can depend.
Though miles apart they're still around,

The friends I've known for many years,
The ones brand new, those yet to find,
With whom I share both laughs and tears.
The years build up the bond that binds.

Some friendships form that never break,
Throughout the years endure and last,
Weather storms, life's give and take,
And share the future, present, past.

I'm grateful for the friends I've known,
I thank the Lord I'm not alone.

AUGUST 29, GOD'S LOVE

I'm grateful Lord I'm blessed write.
I pray it's pleasing in Your sight.
Lord guide my thoughts, show me the way,
That I might spread Your love each day.

I pray Your love and peace abound.
May others hear, find sweet the sound.
May words I pen help others see,
You gave Your life to set them free.

In You I've found abundant life.
You walk with me through toil and strife.
You fill my soul with joy and peace.
Eternal love will never cease.

For you who read, I lift in prayer.
I pray you find God's love and care.

AUGUST 30, ENDURING LOVE

Poems keep swirling around in my head,
Emerging from somewhere inside of my soul.
They come while I'm sitting or resting in bed.
It seems I'm not always the one in control.

I pray that I'm sharing God's love from above,
Capturing truth as I'm writing each word,
Reflecting its essence and writing with love,
Attempting in lyrics to write what I've heard.

As I lyrically share and express what I learn,
I pray I'm effective and help others see
The love of the Lord is not something to earn.
The Lord paid the ransom for you and for me.

God's Word still remains even pierced by a nail.
His love will forever endure and prevail.

AUGUST 31, A GENTLE DAWN

That early morning time of day,
The birds sing out with mellow song
Announcing dawn is on the way.
I sip my coffee black and strong.

I gently rock and feel the breeze.
It brushes gently on my face
And winds its way up through the trees.
The leaves respond, a leisure pace.

The sun begins to share its light.
The clouds reflect its early glow,
That twilight time, the end of night,
A time of day I cherish so.

A time to read, reflect, and pray
Before I start another day.

SEPTEMBER 1, LEARNING TO HEAR

There is sound all around me not meant for the ear.
If I let my heart listen, there's so much to hear.
If I dare to be open to what I might find,
It's then I discover a love that is kind.

In order to listen and hear with my heart
Developing patience is where I must start.
A dose of humility, once it is found,
Will help my heart listen, attuned to the sound.

As I learn how to listen, to love, and to care,
Hope will endure when the world seems unfair.
If I patiently listen, the truth will be heard.
Inside of my soul I'll absorb every word.

It's not what the world has to offer to me,
But rather God's truth that will set my heart free.

SEPTEMBER 2, GLOW

Like a firefly's glow dims when confined to a jar,
Sometimes we get stuck and forget who we are.
We're each one unique, and we work to refine
Our God given talents to learn how to shine.

Sometimes in our struggles our light seems to dim.
We need oil in our lamps for those days life is grim.
Prepare in the good times that God brings our way,
The sunshine He sends us to brighten our day.

We each have a purpose, a role to fulfill.
Sometimes life is hard when we're climbing a hill.
But the view from the top makes the climb seem worthwhile.
In every direction see beauty for miles.

I pray you find beauty and purpose in life.
May your talents shine brightly in spite of the strife.

SEPTEMBER 3, FALL LEAVES

As leaves begin to show their age,
Take on a slightly different hue,
We know they've reached a different stage,
No longer young, bright green and new.

We know they'll usher in the fall,
Once more with brilliant colors glow,
Leave one more summer to recall,
Another winter yet to know.

I'm grateful for another year,
You've given me a life this long.
I know the fall of life is here.
I pray my faith in You stays strong.

Lord let Your colors shine through me,
Reflect Your light, help others see.

SEPTEMBER 4, AUTUMN

Autumn reminds me that winter is near.
It's time to prepare as some winters are long,
Make sure that my faith is engaged and in gear.
Sometimes there's a winter that's bitter and strong.

Like squirrels who gather their food in the fall,
I know that the winter will blast me once more.
Surviving past winters will help me stand tall.
Some winters are brutal and hard to ignore.

Troubles like winters are just part of life.
I pray that I'm ready, prepared when they come.
I'm grateful for time to prepare for the strife.
Lord give me the strength that I'm not overcome.

Lord give me the courage and the faith to endure,
To trust in Your love, You are faithful and pure.

SEPTEMBER 5, A YEAR OF POEMS

I wrote enough poems to last a whole year.
It helped me to capture what's buried inside.
It's better to bare it with poems sincere,
Than keeping the feelings and letting them hide.

Feelings like mushrooms can grow in the dark,
Some of them poisonous, strange, or bizarre.
Pulled up by the roots they may still leave a mark,
Time will bring healing, just leaving a scar.

Along with the strange I discovered some love,
A deep-rooted faith, a reflection of light,
A joy that's within me that comes from above,
A knowledge that someday there'll be no more night.

I pray as I share that my words remain true,
That my verses convey a reflection of You.

SEPTEMBER 6, OLD TIMER

In terms of my poetry, I'm an old timer.
I've not written long as I started quite late,
But my verses are metered, you'd call me a rhymer.
When verses start flowing, I don't hesitate.

The thought or the image that comes from my heart
I render by painting with words in my head.
Sometimes it's a landscape that grows once I start.
Sometimes it's emotion that needs to be fed.

I'm amazed at the images captured by words,
The beauty that poets have shared through the years.
The rendering's different each time it is heard,
The hope and the joy that we find among tears.

I pray that my poetry lingers a while,
Finds its way to a heart that's in need of a smile.

SEPTEMBER 7, A MENTOR

A mentor is weathered yet seasoned by time,
And graced by maturity, lessons well earned.
Discovered the peaks and each step of the climb.
Is able to share all the wisdom discerned.

A mentor's not perfect but willing to share
From the reservoir filled by the journey through life.
The message falls softly, is spoken with care,
Learned from experience, troubles, and strife.

We all need a mentor who touches our heart.
One who can help us when reading God's word.
Help us find answers and wisdom impart.
Help us to see, understand what we heard.

I pray you have someone in whom you confide,
With whom you can pray and is close by your side.

SEPTEMBER 8, LIFE

It's not so important how long that we live,
But rather the value of what we can give.
Sometimes just a gesture or even a smile
Can let someone know that they're valued, worthwhile.

It's amazing the impact our words can convey,
The way that we act and the things that we say.
The life that we're given is more than a test.
Finding ways to bless others is our daily quest.

"It's more blessed to give than it is to receive,"
Is a pathway to joy if we dare to believe.
Each life is a gift that was given to share,
To help out a neighbor in need of our care.

As we reach out to others and kindness embrace,
We're sharing God's love and His mercy and grace.

SEPTEMBER 9, MORNING PRAYER

The rhymes are now slowing, not writing each day.
It's much more important to take time to pray.
I'm grateful to God that I still have my wife,
Someone to love me, we're wedded for life.

I pray for my family, pray for each friend,
"Lord keep them all healthy, when hurt may they mend."
I pray they know joy and Your peace from above.
I pray they seek wisdom but most of all love.

I pray for our nation, that people may heal,
Both inside and out help the way that they feel.
I pray that the wisdom our forefathers shared
Be taught to our children, they'll know that we cared.

I pray that Your light will allow us to see.
Help us to follow You, starting with me.

SEPTEMBER 10, JOURNAL OF LOVE

In this world I see evil, it's on full display.
I see it in headlines, on news every day.
I try to find wisdom that's found in God's word,
To read His word daily, absorb what I've heard.

So many are hurting, and suffering wrongs,
Inflicted through evil pretending it's strong.
Lord help us to turn and to seek after light,
Each day be devoted to doing what's right.

Lord help me seek righteousness, teach me to live,
Help me distribute the love that You give.
In Your word I find beauty, You fill me with hope.
Help me find ways to do more than just cope.

Lord help me to journal, point others to You,
Capture in verses Your love that is true.

SEPTEMBER 11, PAUSE AND PRAY

When life's overwhelming, no wind in my sails,
I pause for a moment and take time to pray.
I remember God loves me and prayer never fails.
I know if I'm open, He'll show me the way.

Sometimes all the messes encountered in life
Can leave me perplexed, I don't understand why.
In the midst of the troubles, the turmoil and strife,
The Lord paints a rainbow across the dark sky.

I don't need all the answers, I just need to trust.
He'll lead me and guide me, protect me in storms.
The Lord is my refuge, the rest turns to dust.
One day I'll be with Him, take on a new form.

This life's a small journey, a short span of time.
My spirit's eternal, God's glory's sublime.

SEPTEMBER 12, POETIC VERSE

Poetic verse sets free my mind,
Allows my heart once more to sing.
My spirit soars, new heights to find,
Glide on the breeze, no need for wings.

Words lift me up, leave cares below,
The rhythm of the flowing sound
Immerses me within the flow.
Lord fill me up, let love abound.

I pray my words help others see.
May they explore inside your Word,
Discover Who can set them free,
Rely on truth, not what they've heard.

I thank you Lord, I know Your love,
One day I'll be with You above.

SEPTEMBER 13, GOD'S PRECIOUS GIFT

Four generations down to you,
God has a plan, He'll see it through.
We treasure you, our little one.
Your precious life has just begun.

We know the plans God has in store
Are just for you, and none before.
He made you perfect in His sight.
Each day we pray you find delight.

Each day you grow and learn and play,
I pray you know God's love each day.
We love you little precious child,
Your eyes, your laugh, your little smile.

You picked a special mom and dad.
We love you too, we're proud and glad.

SEPTEMBER 14, PRAYING FRIENDS

I thank the Lord for friends who pray
Not just for me but others too.
I also pray for you today.
I pray God richly blesses you.

Praise God for faithful caring friends.
We share good times and laugh a bit.
Upon your prayers I can depend.
I also love your smile, your wit.

Your heart is strong and also kind.
I'm grateful that our journey's shared.
Good friends like you are hard to find.
We lift each other up in prayer.

I'm grateful that we share God's love
And both will live with Him above.

SEPTEMBER 15, MELODIES

Rhythm and lyrics I easily find
Just lingering somewhere inside of my mind.
I'm lacking a melody, not quite a song,
I don't hear the music, find notes that belong.

If one day the melodies start to arise
Like the rhyme and the rhythm, I'll be quite surprised.
I'm blessed with the thoughts and the words to impart
The lyrical verses that form in my heart.

I'm grateful to capture the lyrics I write,
But also, I yearn, and I pray that they might
Grow up to be more than just words that I say.
Perhaps find a melody, marry someday.

The music would play, and the bells would be rung.
The lyrics and melody then could be sung.

SEPTEMBER 16, CHOOSE LIGHT

Why settle for a basement life
Where little light is found,
Allow the stress brought on by strife
To keep you burdened down?

The Lord provides a better way
He'll bear your heavy load.
Call out to Him, take time to pray,
Then choose a different road.

Walk with the Lord and read His Word,
Discover joy inside.
Then celebrate. Your prayers are heard.
You're free, no more to hide.

The basement is no place for you.
Trust God, His Word is true.

SEPTEMBER 17, ACTIVE MINDS

How can I articulate my feelings into words,
Assemble them so they make sense,
   if someone were to read?
And even if the thoughts I pen are never to be heard,
At least I've let my feelings bloom, not just remain a seed.

An active mind when exercised like any muscle grows.
The nourishment that it requires comes in from all around,
To help it probe the vast domain, discover what it knows.
A healthy mind is one well fed, with roots in fertile ground.

A mind well-tuned and exercised can do most anything.
An idle mind seems such a waste, at least provide a book.
Choose healthy food from history,
   see what the classics bring,
God's written Word will stretch the mind,
   it's worth the time to look.

A mind that's fed unhealthy junk can quickly go astray,
So many people all around with messages to sell.
Be careful to evaluate what others have to say,
Good motives or an evil heart, it's often hard to tell.

I recommend God's written word, it's healthy and it's true.
It helps my mind expand and grow,
   keep learning something new.

SEPTEMBER 18, THE GATHERING

Some call us old codgers, us elderly men.
We gather together, share scriptures and prayers.
There's nothing like sharing some time with a friend.
Our spirits are lifted along with our cares.

The Lord has provided us decades of life.
We've gathered some wisdom, most learned the hard way.
We've had a long journey, both good times and strife.
We're grateful and blessed as we greet a new day.

I pray as we're reading and hearing God's Word,
That His Spirit is working inside of our heart.
I pray when we leave that we've not only heard,
But truly know peace that will never depart.

You've made us all different, we each have a role.
I pray Lord Your Blessing on each unique soul.

SEPTEMBER 19, SUNDAY MORNING PRAYER

It's Sunday Lord, a day of rest.
I pray this day I'm at my best.
A day to read, to hear Your Word,
To lift a prayer and know it's heard.

I'm still amazed You care for me.
You lift me up and set me free.
You give me peace inside my heart,
You're always there and won't depart.

I lift up those who need Your care,
Those sick and hurting everywhere.
Lord heal them body, mind and soul,
That once again they may be whole.

I pray as summer fades to fall,
We turn to You and heed Your call.
I pray this day the tide will turn,
Lord grant us wisdom to discern.

SEPTEMBER 20, THOSE WHO REMAIN

God formed us all and gave us breath,
Made in His image yet unique,
Live earthly days until our death.
Beyond the grave we cannot peek.

Our days we spend upon the earth,
Each one ordained, each time and place.
We each have gifts bestowed at birth.
We all comprise the human race.

Instead of using gifts for good,
Discovering how best to live,
Our talents seldom understood,
There's so much more that we could give.

I long to see the hate recede,
See wickedness begin to fade,
See love abound and good succeed,
Yet evil lurks, seeks to invade.

I'm sensing that the end is near.
Abruptly we'll be snatched away.
Those who remain and linger here
Will get their wish, no one to pray.

SEPTEMBER 21, HEARTS WRITE

A poem's something done alone,
A quiet pensive thoughtful fare.
It's not for those with hearts of stone,
Or those shut down, not prone to share.

One's poetry comes from the heart.
It's best when shared from deep inside.
Don't wait to find a place to start,
Just share your heart, let nothing hide.

Sometimes I write and also pray.
At first, I share my heart with God.
It's then I find the words to say.
Perhaps He gives my heart a prod.

I urge you too to pray and write.
I pray you find God's love and light.

SEPTEMBER 22, PENNING WORDS

I pray I discern when my writing should end.
Are there any more words that my heart needs to share?
What more would I say sitting down with a friend,
Or in rhymes shared with others when I'm not aware?

I pray that the rhythm and rhyme of each line
Like a balm soothes the heart for a moment or two.
May the Lord bless the words, turning water to wine.
May His love in my soul be found also in you.

I can write from my heart as I pen words each day.
I can share what I find, what I read in His Word.
As I try to explain, use the right words to say,
I cannot control if the message is heard.

Lord help me keep writing, provide those who read,
As long as my words are still meeting a need.

SEPTEMBER 23, ONE DAY AT A TIME

I seldom see clearly God's purpose for me.
The pathway behind me is marred with debris.
The road up ahead is so hard to discern.
One day at a time is not easy to learn.

The Lord doesn't give me a roadmap for life,
Or allow me to choose, or to filter the strife.
I've learned I can trust Him to show me the way.
He gives me the courage, enough for today.

I pray that today I can rest and let go,
Just live in the present, there's no more to know.
I can rest in the knowledge that God's in control,
I can trust Him with everything, even my soul.

One day I'll see clearly when this journey's done,
The struggles are over, the battle's been won.

SEPTEMBER 24, SHARING FAITH

I share my faith with words of rhyme.
I pray they last beyond my time.
I pray they help another see,
A glimpse into eternity.

Our lives are brief upon this earth,
Our days are numbered from our birth.
Created by the Master's hand,
We cannot fully understand.

Much like a child we want control,
Define our life, attain a goal,
Then in a flash we're at the end.
I pray by then the Lord's your friend.

I pray you've known His love for years,
Walked by His side through joys and tears.

SEPTEMBER 25, WORDS ECHO

The words we write or speak today
Leave echoes that forever stay.
They linger in the cosmic dust
That forms the past, provides it thrust.

Some words can hurt, bring hate or fear,
While others comfort, draw us near.
Why fill the air with words so dark,
When words can be a meadow lark?

May words of comfort be the sound
That echoes hope where grief is found.
May words of love cut through the hate.
Reach out, embrace, it's not too late.

I pray the words I write ring true,
Convey the love of God to you.

SEPTEMBER 26, IN CONTROL

But our God is in the heavens; He does whatever He pleases.
Psalm 115:3

God needs no counsel, He has full control.
He does as He pleases, no need to explain.
He knows of our heartache, He's there to console.
If I trust Him in hard times instead of complain,

If in faith I can praise Him when things seem so wrong,
If I trust in His love when my world falls apart,
Then through trials when I'm tested, I pray I'll grow strong.
I pray when it's over I'll have a fresh start.

Troubles last through the evening, but morning brings light.
The troubles in this life one day will be done.
I only see glimpses, one day I'll gain sight.
One day I will see Him, give thanks to His Son.

Even in hard times when things go awry,
I trust Him to love me, no need to ask why.

SEPTEMBER 27, MEND AND SOAR

If I stay down, choose not to soar,
I'm missing out, there's so much more.
I cannot fit inside a mold,
Nor just sit back, watch life unfold.

Is it a waste of thought or time
To share my heart and soul in rhyme?
I pray my verse helps others cope,
And reaches out to offer hope.

I pray my words help others sing,
Someone who needs a mended wing,
A little help before they fly,
Before they soar into the sky.

I pray God blesses you this day.
I pray your hurts soon fade away.

SEPTEMBER 28, PASSING THROUGH

I never know if this will be
  my final parting rhyme,
The day the Lord will call my name,
  provide a different home.
If today will mark the end
  of this my earthly time,
My spirit, soul set free again,
  throughout the heavens roam.

I value all the friends I've made
  throughout my earthly stay.
I know that I'm a stranger here,
  that I'm just passing through.
My home is with the Lord on high
  and I'll be called away.
That final phase provides for me
  a life forever new.

I thank the Lord each day I'm here
  for this my time on earth,
The beauty of creation that
  God put me here to see.
I'm grateful for each day I've spent,
  each day beyond my birth.
I'm grateful for each day of life the Lord has given me.

When my final chapter's done,
   there's no more left to tell,
I pray that I've accomplished all
   the things I should have done.
I pray that I have pleased the Lord
   and I have lived it well,
When He calls and says to me,
   "It's time, come home my son."

Lord lead the way and teach me Lord
   each day to follow you.
Help me Lord to seize each day,
   know things I've left to do.

SEPTEMBER 29, WE YOUR PEOPLE

Lord grant us words to spread Your love,
Refresh like dew from up above,
That penetrate a hardened heart,
Words that cling and won't depart.

Your love we sorely need today,
So many folks who've lost their way,
Confused by rhetoric gone wrong.
It's time to sing once more Your song,

A song of love, a song of grace,
A song that fills an empty space,
A loneliness, a hurt, a fear.
Your song of love I pray we hear.

Lord touch our hearts, once more renew
Our spirit Lord, drawn close to You.
Lord grant us wisdom, words to share,
Help us, Your people, show we care.

SEPTEMBER 30, DRAW NEAR

I don't cause the sun to come up every morn.
I don't make the clouds and the rain in the sky.
I don't cause a kernel to sprout, produce corn.
What gives me the right to demand to know why?

I'm not the creator who formed me at birth,
Who put every star in the sky in its place.
I'm sure there's a reason I'm here on this earth.
I pray that the Lord, full of beauty and grace,

Will guide and direct me as I find my way,
Help me find wisdom each day as I write,
Help me draw closer to God every day,
Help me dig deep, let my heart provide sight.

As the sun begins rising, I pause and draw near.
Lord help me to listen, discern, and to hear.

OCTOBER 1, WHATEVER COMES

Another week is near complete.
Sometimes life's tough but won't defeat.
I will survive what life may bring.
My heart still finds a way to sing.

Whatever comes throughout the year,
I won't give in to doubt and fear.
My body's aged, my soul's still strong,
I reach inside to find a song.

I find the words to bring me cheer,
Perhaps words others need to hear.
I pray we find the courage, strength
To share with others what we think,

Share words of kindness, blessings, hope,
Help others learn new ways to cope.
We all have troubles come our way,
Reach out to help someone today.

OCTOBER 2, FORMING WORDS

When words flow together, express how I feel,
Get out in the open no longer concealed,
My soul finds some comfort by forming each word.
With rhyme and with rhythm perhaps they'll be heard.

There's nothing profound in the words that I write.
It's the simple and soothing in which I delight.
Some people journal to share what's inside,
To capture their essence, in others confide.

I'm drawn to the beat of the drums in my head,
The words in formation as though they are led.
Sometimes I'm conductor, the instruments play.
Together in harmony words can convey

The feelings inside me my heart wants to share.
I pray they help others find peace not despair.

OCTOBER 3, SLEEP WELL

I pray that these verses can help you to sleep,
Find rest in a slumber that's peaceful and deep.
As your body releases the tension it holds,
The muscles relax, loose their grip and unfold.

I pray all confusion that stirs in your head
Will fade through the pillow and out of the bed.
I pray that the images, thoughts that remain
Bring sweet sounding music with every refrain.

I pray in your dreams that you're floating and free,
Enamored with beauty in all that you see.
I pray that your body finds rest and can heal,
As you're drifting above there's no pain you can feel.

I pray you find peace as you sleep through the night,
A deep restful slumber 'til morning's first light.

OCTOBER 4, CHOICES

Each day, each year brings many roads,
So many paths from which to choose.
Some choices come with heavy loads,
We paint our life with many hues.

Some roads in life we choose to take
Have exit ramps placed far apart.
A choice is made, a dumb mistake,
See clearly now it wasn't smart.

Each choice we make has consequence.
The choice is made, we pay a price,
Sometimes much more than just a pence,
Another choice, like sugar, spice.

Wise choices lead to better days.
God's guiding light removes the haze.

OCTOBER 5, JOURNEYS

As a youth I would roam in the woods with my friends.
We'd build cabins and forts from old logs made of pine.
Life seemed much easier, simpler back then,
Each day an adventure, no reason to whine.

As we got a bit older, we'd sleep overnight
In the woods on a bedroll out under the stars,
With pine straw for pillows, a lantern for light.
Our canteens for water were old mason jars.

We'd talk about life and the places we'd go,
Share stories and tales and the things that we'd heard,
Look up at the stars and the moon with its glow,
Hear sounds of the crickets, the song of a bird.

In my mind I can journey to times in my past.
As I relive the moments, they linger and last.

OCTOBER 6, DEPTH

I cannot determine the length of my life,
Nor have much control of the size of the strife.
My focus instead is the depth of my soul.
In the days that I live, that's within my control.

As I reach out to others my soul can expand,
Find ways to touch others, extending my hand.
Not all will respond but at least I can try.
On this journey through life, love's not something we buy.

A spring that is flowing from deep in the ground,
A love that's refreshing, how soothing the sound.
I pray I share love from the depths of my heart,
Reflecting the Lord who will never depart.

I pray you find love in the words that I write,
A sprinkle of wisdom, a dash of insight.

OCTOBER 7, LASTING TREASURES

The image before us comes in through our eyes.
The sounds all around us we gather with ears.
As we see with the heart, we begin to grow wise.
As we learn how to listen, we truly can hear.

The Lord works in our lives in mysterious ways.
He molds us and shapes us and helps us to see
His love's everlasting throughout all our days.
Why waste time in bondage when we could be free?

Why focus on things of this world that don't last?
Our life on this earth like a vapor will fade.
The present so quickly fades into the past.
Our spirit lives on though our bodies degrade.

Lord help me to see and to hear with my heart,
To focus on treasures that never depart.

OCTOBER 8, WHEN SHADOWS COME

During times when the shadows cross over my soul,
I wonder if writing's a blessing or curse.
I find disappointing events that unfold,
And yet I keep sharing words written in verse.

Perhaps it is helpful to write it all down,
Both the good and the bad, everything that I feel.
Should I only share smiles, and keep silent the frown?
I think it's important to always be real.

The Lord knows when I'm weary, in need of His peace.
He offers to help me to carry the load.
He steadies my soul, and my burdens decrease.
With Him at my side I can walk any road.

In those times when the shadows of life cover me,
I can call on the Lord, He will set my soul free.

OCTOBER 9, WORDS IN A BOTTLE

Should I capture the rhymes that erupt in my head?
I write them but should I ignore them instead?
I never know when, even who, they will reach,
Like words in a bottle washed up on a beach.

One day someone finds it all covered with sand,
Wonders, "Is this a treasure I hold in my hand?
"Perhaps an old pirate has left me a map."
Holds up the bottle and gives it a tap.

Is that how it works when words float through the web,
Just bobbing and waiting for someone to grab?
Unlike a bottle that's found by just one,
Words stay on the net and are never quite done.

The words that you've found that you're reading this day,
Means you have been touched, it's for you that I pray.
I pray you find peace and know joy in your heart.
Be blessed by the Lord who will never depart.

OCTOBER 10, HOPE

Hope provides courage and patience to wait.
The journey's not over, it's not yet too late.
Don't get discouraged when life seems unfair,
But reach out to others and show love and care.

By going through valleys encountered in life,
We learn from the hard times, the troubles, and strife.
We build up endurance and strength for each day,
Some of them sunny while others are gray.

Hope requires faith, an abundance of love,
A spirit inside that is sent from above.
Hope is not something to see, feel, or taste,
And yet it's essential, not something to waste.

I'm grateful for hope and the faith to believe
In the Lord who's eternal, who never will leave.

OCTOBER 11, GOODBYE TO A FRIEND

It's hard to let go, say goodbye to a friend,
Sad that their days on this earth had to end.
So many fond mem'ries remain in our heart,
They'll linger forever and never depart.

Remember the good times enjoyed in the past,
Cherish those memories, hold to them fast.
I'm grateful for friends, we have all shared so much.
We lean on each other, no need for a crutch.

Together we honor the life of our friend,
Though no longer with us his life will not end.
In heaven he's frolicking, happy, carefree,
Beholding the beauty, there's so much to see.

We'll see him again just inside heaven's gate.
Together with Jesus, it's not long to wait.

OCTOBER 12, HARD TIMES

Why should we carry our troubles alone?
The Lord is our strength, He is steady and strong.
Why do we tarry, put off, and postpone?
He's not likely to ask us, "What took you so long?"

We need help when the hard times in life come our way.
We're not made for those burdens too heavy to bear.
That load can be lifted, just take time to pray.
He carries the burdens we're willing to share.

The troubles will come, some will linger, remain.
Others the Lord will remove, take away.
It's not about winning or losing or gain,
The troubles we face as we go through each day,

But rather the faith that we build up inside,
As we walk with the Lord and remain at His side.

OCTOBER 13, MOMENTS I CHERISH

Why complicate life chasing rainbows or clouds?
A life that is simple, away from the crowds,
A chair on the patio, time spent alone,
With no interruptions, not even a phone,

Time to write poetry, contemplate life,
Sharing my words, spending time with my wife,
Sipping hot coffee and petting my pup,
Seeing the colors that come with sunup,

Watching the birds as they swoop through the air,
Feeling the breeze as it ruffles my hair,
Sun highlighting colors of butterfly wings,
The gentle soft sound of the chime as it rings,

Reading God's Word, bare my soul as I pray,
Are moments I cherish to start off my day.

OCTOBER 14, UNIQUELY MADE

God skillfully made us, we're each His delight.
He formed us uniquely with love and with care.
Our soul and our spirit so clear in His sight,
Our innermost being, He's fully aware.

We each have potential that God placed inside
To know and to love Him, then use what He gave
To share love with others, we're not made to hide.
It's only a body we leave in a grave.

As I learn to serve others, less focused on me,
I find myself happy, no room for despair.
As I learn to love others my soul is set free.
God's Spirit inside me is meant to be shared.

Lord guide and direct me and show me your will.
You gave me a purpose I pray I fulfill.

OCTOBER 15, FOLLOW

I pray I can listen and follow God's will,
Be fully aware of what God has to say.
Perhaps there's a mission he'd have me fulfill.
I pray I can follow and not lose my way.

I pray for God's guidance that's found in His Word.
I pray that His Spirit will help me to hear.
I pray that His message will clearly be heard.
May I hear with my heart and not just with my ears.

In order to follow, then first I must read.
In order to hear I must open my heart,
Be willing to follow wherever He leads.
Lord grant me discernment to know where to start.

Lord help me to follow, each day is brand new.
I pray that each day I draw closer to You.

OCTOBER 16, CHERISH THE DAYS

Fall's in the air with a chilly north wind.
The summer reluctantly comes to an end.
A taste of the winter that soon will unfold,
Sometimes bringing with it a fierce bitter cold.

The winters get harder each year to endure.
Aging comes naturally needing no cure.
Our winter's upon us that last stage of life.
We've grown old together as husband and wife.

One of us likely will be left behind
Remembering days that were tender and kind,
Recalling the places, the memories shared,
The everyday moments, the love and the care.

We'll cherish the days for us both that remain,
As we finish together life's final refrain.

OCTOBER 17, A LITTLE KINDNESS

With so many lonely, or hurting, or sad,
I pray over time they find reasons for glad.
I pray there is someone to speak a kind word,
Someone to listen, acknowledge they've heard.

A kindness performed out of love from the heart
Can begin someone's journey to find a fresh start.
Even a smile, just a touch or a hug
Is better than turning away with a shrug.

A little compassion can go a long way
Towards lifting the spirit of someone today.
Don't let opportunity slip through your hand,
Perhaps a small favor, it needn't be grand.

I try to share kindness with words that I write,
Words that I pray are reflecting God's light.

OCTOBER 18, GOD'S WORD

God's Word, the Bible, always true,
God shared His Word through quite a few.
Those trusted men wrote down the words
Empowered to capture what they heard.

I thank the Lord His Word's preserved,
And for His gift no one deserved.
He sent His Son to make a way
For us to come to God and pray.

He sent His Son that we might live
A gift that only He could give.
He came to earth as flesh and bone,
We could not reach Him on our own.

The Word God shared will never die.
Some day with Him we'll soar and fly.

OCTOBER 19, PAINTING WORDS

I love to paint a scene with words
That comes alive when read or heard.
I love to capture thoughts in rhyme
Before they fade away with time.

Like sun and clouds mix brilliant hues
Each morning brings me something new.
Scenes from my soul mix in my mind.
Sometimes the words are hard to find.

Some swirl inside as gentle breeze
That can be felt or seen in trees.
Others come more like a storm.
I hold on tight and let words form.

We've all been through a tough few years.
We've shed some tears and conquered fears.
Some days it seemed were truly blessed,
While other days seemed like a test.

Perhaps with words I can convey
What bubbles up inside each day.
Perhaps, if shared, the words will last,
Provide a glimpse into the past.

I pray I always find some good,
That scenes I paint are understood.

OCTOBER 20, REACHING OUT

I love to pen poems and share what I write.
It's my way of spreading God's word and His light.
If you'd like to hear me read rhymes for a while,
I'd be happy to come, share my rhymes with a smile.

I can tailor my readings to match with a theme,
Or I can pick rhymes that I share with your team.
It's a joy to reach out, pray my words touch your heart.
It's always a pleasure and hard to depart.

I've written some picture books, chapter books too,
And also, some poetry books just for you.
Let me know if you want me to bring a few books.
Some want a signed copy while others just look.

Reach out if you'd like to arrange, set a date.
Engagements are limited, don't wait too late.

OCTOBER 21, WE MEET ON A THURSDAY

We share our hearts, our lives, our prayer
Surrounded by good men who care.
We know the Lord, His will, His way,
We trust the Lord for each new day.

There's more to learn as we are taught
God's Word brings insight, wisdom, thought.
Each day His Word is fresh and new,
We see more life He's led us through.

We're grateful to ladies, those meeting next door,
They bless us with cookies and goodies galore,
Some of them married to gents in our group,
Some use a walker or walk with a stoop,

We're blessed to still have them as part of our life.
We value each day we've been blessed by a wife.

OCTOBER 22, PURE JOY

My soul to heaven soon will rise,
I'll look into my Savior's eyes.
I'll find pure joy, fulfilled at last,
I'll know His love, discard the past.

No need for fear, all evil's done.
We'll celebrate. The battle's won.
I'll lift my voice, give God my praise.
New revelations will amaze,

To know pure love forevermore,
See sights I never seen before.
His majesty is all around,
Angelic chorus, what a sound.

My soul will rise and leave this place,
Beyond the bounds of time and space.

OCTOBER 23, INWARD REFLECTIONS

I don't have to chisel my words into rock.
Though I write on a tablet, it's charged in a dock.
No matter how captured, how poems unfold,
Sharing words from the heart I pray never grows old.

Poetic expression reflects what's inside.
Words keep me humble there's no room for pride.
I'm amazed at how easily words seem to flow.
How long I'll keep rhyming I've no way to know.

Sometimes I'm up early with no one around.
I type on a touch screen, just silence, no sound.
Sometimes in a lobby, I'm part of a crowd,
Just capturing words, not reciting out loud.

If rhyming's old fashioned, no longer in vogue,
Then call me a rebel, and label me rogue.
I pray I write words that can linger a while.
Soothing and comforting's always in style.

I pray as I share, in some small way assist,
An inward reflection that's hard to resist.
I pray you find harmony, peace in your heart.
God's love that's eternal will never depart.

OCTOBER 24, WHO IS GOD?

How can I capture my God with a rhyme?
Omnipotent Master beyond space and time.
Omniscient, all knowing, created all things,
We're made in His image, to Him our soul sings.

Omnipresent, sees all things, throughout time and space,
And yet extends love, we are saved by His grace.
Beyond comprehension, the depths of His love,
Who came as a man from His place up above.

I'm careful to never put God in a box,
Not even cathedrals of stone cut from rocks.
Not even the angels who circle His throne
Can see all the facets, so much to be known.

My God is my Father, my Savior and friend,
His love is forever, no bounds and no end.

OCTOBER 25, OBSCURITY

Though my rhymes may remain in obscurity,
I'd rather pen words with sincerity,
Than rising to fame writing pages of filth
Consumed by the masses ignoring the guilt.

If the size of my audience comes to expand,
I pray that it comes by the touch of God's hand.
I pray that I serve what God puts on my plate.
God grant me the wisdom and patience to wait.

I pray I continue to write from my heart.
I pray that my passion will never depart.
I pray I will always with words I convey,
Be a blessing to others who read them someday.

I pray that I've listened. I pray that I've heard.
I pray what I write is aligned with God's Word.

OCTOBER 26, GOD'S IN CONTROL

The storms and the clouds get so dark in the sky,
We keep searching for answers and want to know why.
There's so much in life that's beyond our control.
We're easily wearied, let worry take hold.

I pray you have faith that you need for today,
That God's in control and will show you the way.
I pray you find peace and relief from your pain.
Sometimes it seems burdens consume us like rain.

I pray you find courage to give God control,
Find comfort and love flowing deep in your soul.
I pray you find rest that your strength can renew.
Your life is not finished, there's more here to do.

I pray that today you find sunshine and light,
Your soul is uplifted, your world is made right.

OCTOBER 27, SOOTHING COMFORT

You are the balm to soothe my soul,
To comfort me as I grow old.
You place inside my heart a song.
Your warm embrace says I belong.

Your Spirit has a home inside,
A special place where love abides.
For now, I know You through a haze.
But when complete these earthly days,

I'll spend eternity with You,
Where everything is fresh and new.
To enter realms now unaware,
Will be a sight beyond compare.

Beyond the bounds of time and space,
I'll find my final resting place.

OCTOBER 28, SATISFIED

When I run ahead without patience to wait,
Thinking I'm in control and in charge of my fate,
I'm not fooling anyone, even myself.
Lord give me the patience to wait on the shelf.

Help me learn satisfaction with what life may bring,
See beauty in simple to help my heart sing,
Find joy in the tiny no matter how small,
Find joy in the daily response to Your call.

Content penning words that with rhythm align,
That point out a truth like a painting or sign,
Sharing God's love a few lines at a time,
I love to write verses that end with a rhyme.

Words float on the web; some appear in a book.
I pray they're a blessing should anyone look.

OCTOBER 29, A GIFT TO SHARE

I'm blessed that a poem's not costly in time.
The words fall together when forming a rhyme.
I gather the thoughts when they form in my head,
Then stitch them together like needle with thread.

I put them together, those snippets of verse,
Then smooth them like butter not lumpy or terse.
Like a spoon full of sugar to sweeten the sound,
I try to put rhythm to words I have found.

I pray that my verses are soothing to hear,
Are heard on the inside not just with your ear.
I pray that they lift you whenever you're low,
Like a gift or a present adorned with a bow.

Perhaps you will share them with someone in need,
Encourage another to do a good deed.

OCTOBER 30, SEASONS OF BLESSINGS

The wind blew the leaves that now cover the ground.
Fall has arrived with a nip in the air.
Those warm summer evenings, nowhere to be found.
Each season arrives with its own special flair.

The seasons of life, a more subtle change,
Those seasons stretch longer but nonetheless come.
I have my regrets, but I would not exchange
The seasons behind me, though youthful are some.

I'm blessed to have lived through a good many years.
I've been many places, seen how others live,
Experienced heart ache and shed a few tears.
I'm blessed that the Lord thinks there's more I can give.

I pray that I'm blessed and can finish life strong
No matter the journey, no matter how long.

OCTOBER 31, A QUIET PLACE

A quiet place to rest and pray
A time to read God's Holy Word
A bit of solitude each day
Inside my heart I pray I've heard

The Lord took time away from crowds
And His disciples listened, learned
In gentle words not spoken loud
He shared with them and they discerned

His words remain for us to read
A daily bread to feed our soul
Both soul and body must be fed
We need God's Word to keep us whole

I pray you have a quiet place
To speak to God and know His grace

NOVEMBER 1, VAST AND DEEP

I'm in awe as I ponder the depth of the sky,
And consider the vastness displayed in the night.
It's beyond understanding the how or the why.
I know I can't measure the length or the height.

I'm grateful for pictures now made of the stars.
The beauty revealed as we probe in the deep.
The orbiting telescopes probing so far,
Collecting the images captured to keep.

Yet the one who created the heavens and earth
Also knows me, every hair on my head.
He knows every moment beginning at birth.
One day I'll be with Him, I've nothing to dread.

Then in His presence at last, I will see,
My eyes fully opened, my spirit set free.

NOVEMBER 2, A SMILE

Sometimes it's the small things that lodge in my heart,
Perhaps just a smile, or a hug, or firm hand.
It's the warmth and the feelings such gestures impart,
Affirming assurance that friends understand.

It takes but an instant to show that we care.
A small act of kindness can go a long way,
And touch a heart deeper than we were aware.
Our words and our actions have much to convey.

If I'm true to myself, and I let others see,
If my heart is reflected by words that I choose,
I find when I share, I learn more about me.
I plan to keep sharing, I've nothing to lose.

I pray as I write that I'm sharing a smile.
Perhaps it will linger and stay for a while.

NOVEMBER 3, SO LITTLE LEARNED

What size is the building for all of the books
It would take to contain what we think we have learned?
But that's only one section, a small little nook,
So much we don't know, so few pages we've turned.

So much about life that we fail to pass on,
Things we could share that we know to be true.
Life's more than inventing more ways to have fun.
It's not about finding more things to accrue.

We came here with nothing, that's how we will leave.
It's not what we gather but what we can give.
I have a creator I know and believe,
Through His Son and His Spirit, I learn how to live.

Don't accept as the truth it's by chance we are here.
God's love is a song that our hearts long to hear.

NOVEMBER 4, STATESMEN

Why do our hearts fill up with hate
To poison minds, invade debate?
Instead of different points of view,
The insults rage and venom spews.

Will statesmen rise to change our ways,
Restore again more civil days?
I long to hear a clear calm voice
Lay out a path, provide a choice.

Lord raise up leaders is my plea,
Wise leadership to keep us free,
Who lead with strength, integrity,
Not filled with pride or vanity,

Who work together, form a plan,
Keep freedom strong throughout our land.

NOVEMBER 5, TOUGH TO LEARN

Some days when I'm down, when I just need a lift,
I remember each day that I live is a gift.
No matter what troubles that each day may bring,
I know there is hope and my heart can still sing.

The morning will dawn, and the sun will still rise.
The storms will move out to reveal the blue skies.
Though cloudy or sunny there's always each day,
A pathway to joy as the Lord leads the way.

I pray you find joy although troubles may come,
Find strength in the chaos as you overcome.
I pray you know peace, may you truly be blessed
With strength to endure when life gives you a test.

We'll get through the storms; the blue skies will return.
The valleys are tough but it's there that we learn.

NOVEMBER 6, FLY HIGHER

God's Word gives me freedom and helps me to fly.
Without it I'm drifting and tossed all about.
Like a kite needs a string to soar high in the sky,
The Lord gives me courage and frees me from doubt.

God's Word gives directions, my guideposts through life.
Why leave on a trip with no access to maps?
Life's a long journey with troubles and strife.
God helps me cross rivers though bridges collapse.

My life has endured through the wind and the storm.
The Lord provides shelter when I'm on the ground.
Though I'm showing some age, a bit tattered and worn,
The Lord through His Word points me towards the profound.

Lord You give me guidance, You help me to soar.
I'm free to fly higher than ever before.

NOVEMBER 7, DISCOVERING GIFTS

To discover the gifts God has placed in our souls,
To give God the glory while doing our best,
Is the key to success and achieving our goals.
If we give them to God, He takes care of the rest.

There's no talent or gift that is worthy of pride.
Each gift is God given created at birth.
Don't boast of a talent but also don't hide.
Give God the glory and cherish its worth.

The Lord provides guidance we need for each day.
If we read His word daily and spend time in prayer,
And follow His leading, He'll show us the way.
He made us and loves us, He always is there.

If we're walking with God and we're seeking His will,
We'll find satisfaction, be truly fulfilled.

NOVEMBER 8, BUSY SCHEDULE

If I am not careful my schedule gets filled,
Gets packed up with items that seem quite worthwhile.
I neglect to take time to just pause and be still,
A time to reflect, to be grateful and smile.

It can easily happen, that holiday rush,
Decorations and shopping, folks darting around.
But it's also important, that quiet and hush,
Allowing some time for the soul with no sound.

A pause to reflect and consider the past
Can help me to focus on what I hold dear.
What to me is important? What really will last?
Will the memories I'm making be cherished next year?

Regardless how cluttered my schedule each day,
It's important to pause, to reflect, and to pray.

NOVEMBER 9, THE CHOICE

The challenges I see today,
The ones that cause such fierce debate,
Seem rooted in the Devil's play.
It's something that I contemplate.

Diversion tactics, "Focus here.
Don't think about a life a stake.
An easy choice, don't shed a tear.
It's quickly done, then you're awake."

The right to choose, live life or die,
Should not be normal, common place,
Without a grave, no one to cry,
No one to see each tiny face.

Consider long and hard the choice,
To end a life that has no voice.

NOVEMBER 10, FREE TO SING

I pray that soon I'll laugh once more.
I'm often much too focused now.
I ponder what life has in store
As though I'm in control somehow.

I do my best, I live each day.
I'm prone to think I'm in control
Of all the things that come my way,
But must admit that's not my role.

God holds my future in His hand.
My trust in Him can set me free.
I need not fully understand,
He'll light my path and help me see.

Embrace the joy the Lord can bring.
God's in control. We're free to sing.

NOVEMBER 11, GOOD ADVICE

There are so many people who peddle advice,
So many solutions, "Just do it and win."
"It's easy, you'll love it, like sugar and spice."
"Make millions, you'll never be wanting again."

If you think that perhaps it's too good to be true,
You're not really sure what you get in return,
Then you're right to ask questions, make sure it's for you,
Investigate fully, be wise and discern.

I'll share what I know that I've learned through the years.
God's my creator. He formed me in love.
I can trust in Him fully. He calms any fears.
One day I'll be with him in heaven above.

You can read for yourself, it is found in God's Word.
It's a gift from the Lord so it's not mine to give,
But a message worth sharing, so everyone's heard.
God's Son paid the price so that others might live.

NOVEMEBR 12, FULFILLMENT

I keep on pursuing the dreams placed inside
By the Lord who provides me a purpose, a goal.
If I follow the pathway that's narrow not wide,
The Lord brings fulfillment that's sweet to the soul.

Sometimes when discouraged, think I should give up,
The Lord gives encouragement, shows me His care.
God's word is refreshing, I drink from its cup.
I find comfort, contentment to write and to share.

I pray that the words that I write, and I pen,
Help you to find what you seek and pursue,
Fulfill all the dreams the Lord's placed deep within,
Attaining the goals the Lord's given to you.

May you know the Lord's blessings each day and each night,
Find joy and contentment, the warmth of His light.

NOVEMBER 13, A DAY OF THANKSGIVING

Thanksgiving's the day when we pause to reflect,
A practice, when busy, we often neglect.
I'm grateful the day's set aside when each fall,
We gather with loved ones and friends to recall

The blessings we've known
   through the months, through the year,
The memories of loved ones, some no longer here,
The moments we cherish, the blessings we've known,
The joys and the tears, and the ways we have grown.

I pray as we gather on Thanksgiving Day,
We share cherished memories, the love they convey.
The children will learn from the stories we share,
Down through generations, compassion and care.

I pray we find others, reach out, share our love,
Share all the blessings received from above.

NOVEMBER 14, REACH OUT

Thanksgiving comes but once a year.
A chilling breeze is in the air
Reminding us that winter's near.
Don't let it catch you unaware.

A pumpkin pie, a turkey roast,
A football game, big screen TV,
No time to waste, no time to coast,
A Friday morning shopping spree.

Take time to pause with grateful heart.
Give thanks to God, hold hands and pray.
To those nearby, those far apart,
Reach out in love this special day.

May gratitude throughout the year
Extend to others far and near.

NOVEMBER 15, GIVE THANKS

God's in control of each day that I live,
Each beat of my heart and each breath that I take.
To the One who made everything what can I give?
Each morning I'm grateful that I can awake.

I give thanks to the Lord who gives life and gives breath.
He's provides for me daily He knows every need.
He's in charge of my life from my birth to my death.
May I honor Him daily with words and with deeds.

It's not about treasures I build up on earth,
But rather the treasures in heaven above.
The things that will last and have value and worth
Are planted by God and are rooted in love.

Lord I offer my prayers and with words I proclaim,
"You are my Lord and I lift up Your name."

NOVEMBER 16, OLD FASHIONED

My words in old fashioned, traditional rhyme
I pray stir some memories, images past,
Bring joy to our hearts perhaps lost for a time,
Reminders of treasures, of things that will last.

The rhyme and the rhythm, though centuries old,
Still warms my heart writing in verses this way.
Life has a way of refining the gold.
I pray words I'm sharing won't soon fade away.

I pray that they linger and stay for a while,
Warm other hearts reading the lines that I pen.
Sometimes it's a sigh, other times it's a smile.
I share what I find when I venture within.

If I share from my heart and not just from my mind,
I pray that it's wisdom I'm leaving behind.

NOVEMBER 17, THANKFUL

As I give thanks Thanksgiving Day,
And bow my head to pause and pray,
Express the thanks inside my heart
For those I love, though far apart,

I pray dear Lord they're safe and warm.
Protect them Lord through all their storms.
For those who risk their lives to serve,
May they be blessed for strength and nerve.

For those who help our children grow,
Inspire them to learn and know,
I'm grateful Lord they help us learn
To open books, to read, discern.

Lord bless those near and far away
With grateful hearts Thanksgiving Day.
Lord fill each heart with joy and love
That radiates from God above.

I'm grateful Lord that we are free
To worship You on bended knee.

NOVEMBER 18, LOVE SHARED

Thanksgiving approaches and Christmas draws near
We're told to be thankful, to be of good cheer,
Yet many are quietly hurting inside.
I pray they find someone in whom to confide.

I pray for the comfort of hugs or a touch,
Expressions of love that can offer so much.
Love is a gift and let's each find a way
To share it with others to brighten their day.

As we share from the heart, we discover great joy
Returned in full measure for us to enjoy.
No matter the number of days that you live,
You'll always know peace if you've learned how to give.

I pray that you know the true source of our love,
The One born in a manger, love sent from above.

NOVEMBER 19, HOMETOWN CHRISTMAS

Celebration of Christmas with folks on the square.
A bit of nostalgia that floats through the air.
Excitement of children, the laughter and smiles,
Santa is coming to greet every child.

See all the vendors with goods on display,
Warm morsels and coffee to start off the day.
The storefronts all lighted, there's pride in the town.
Warm tidings of Christmas, a wonderful sound,

As carolers share, with their voices they sing
The songs of the season, good tidings they bring.
The sun will be setting as we light the tree
The twinkle and sparkle exciting to see.

I pray that your Christmas is special this year,
As you spend time with friends and with those who are near.

NOVEMBER 20, PAINTING WITH WORDS

Sometimes when I write, I feel over exposed.
My heart and my soul are not properly clothed.
I write what I'm feeling, I search for what's there,
Find words to paint pictures that help me to share.

I pray that by sharing, by painting in word,
That others see clearly, the picture's not blurred,
That others find comfort, are soothed by the sound,
As I find a way to express what I've found.

Sometimes when I'm searching, I find some despair,
The feeling that things in this life are not fair,
But I also find faith and some joy mixed with love.
I'm covered with peace that descends like a dove.

Despite all the struggles that this life may bring,
Love still abides and my heart can still sing.

NOVEMBER 21, A THANKSGIVING PRAYER

We're grateful Lord, we've been so blessed,
You comfort us in times of test,
You give us peace when troubles flare.
We know Your love. You're always there.

We pray for those who've suffered loss,
Laid heavy burdens at the cross.
I pray Your love will lift them up,
Refreshing waters fill their cup.

We're grateful Lord for loved ones near,
Those cherished friends to us so dear.
We pray for them some near, some far,
Lord help them glow, shine like a star.

I pray our gratitude this day
Will linger Lord, not fade away.

NOVEMBER 22, BEFORE THE DAWN

There's not yet early morning light
In darkness still before the dawn
Soon morning sun will end the night
Awake a bird, a squirrel, a fawn

A winter's eve comes to an end
The sound of silence fills the air
Another day will soon begin
What it will bring I'm unaware

The coffee's hot inside my cup
The thoughts well up inside my mind
Upon my lap a loving pup
My words spill out to form the lines

A quiet time to read and pray
Pen soothing rhyme to start my day

NOVEMBER 23, CHERISHED MEMORIES

Thanksgiving's behind us and Christmas draws near,
A time to draw close to the ones we hold dear,
A time to give thanks for the birth of a King,
A time to make music, to let our hearts sing.

The joy of the season will mix with the sad,
Reminders of loved ones, the good times we had.
We cherish the love we still have in our heart,
Those no longer with us, for now, we're apart.

Each year brings new ways to show others we care,
To find opportunities, ways we can share.
Sometimes it's a visit to see an old friend,
Or perhaps it's a card with a note that we send.

It's a time to find ways we can reach out in love,
Share mem'ries with those who have loved ones above.

NOVEMBER 24, OLD MEN AND STORIES

Old men share stories, they tell of the past,
The stories from childhood that linger and last.
They've lived a full life but aren't likely to boast.
They share about life, things that matter the most.

If you're privileged to listen to stories from men
Who've lived a long time and remember back when,
You'll learn about history not found in a book.
You'll learn about valor, the courage it took.

You'll learn from the stories the old men will tell,
They loved God and country, they served us all well.
The cost of our freedom took many away.
They carved out the future we're living today.

It's an honor to hear all the stories they share.
Their wisdom is precious, like gold it is rare.

NOVEMBER 25, COLD WINTER DAY

This winter weather's Arctic blast
Brought out the coats and leather gloves
The forecast says that it won't last
Soon back to freezing or above

A single digit plunge of cold
Not often felt around these parts
In future years the stories told
No doubt include this winter's start

In wind the powdered flurries blew
They could not cling to frozen ground
Like birds on wings, they soared and flew
Not here to stay they're homeward bound

I'm grateful for a place to stay
For heat and warmth this winter day

NOVEMBER 26, BE WISE

Words can be passionate, strong and sincere,
Persuasively spoken and easy to hear,
But under the surface the motives are wrong.
It's more about power, exciting a throng.

Beware of an eloquent passionate speech
That tries to entice you, persuade you, beseech.
Examine the motives, the spirit, the heart.
Understand what you're doing before you take part.

Be wise as a serpent and take time to pray.
Examine the scriptures and see what they say.
Seek Godly counsel from friends who are wise.
Words spoken convincingly still can be lies.

I pray for wise leaders whose motives are pure,
Who love God and country to help us endure.

NOVEMBER 27, THE PRESENT

We cannot know which day's our last,
Go back in time, or change the past.
The present is our point of view.
Each day is fresh, each day is new.

It's up to us to seize the day,
Keep moving forward, find our way.
Each day is formed by how we live,
By what we learn, by what we give.

Each day we live by faith and hope,
Allow our souls to more than cope,
Content with what each may bring,
Stirs joy inside to help us sing.

Each day provides a brand-new start
To share the love that's in our heart.

NOVEMBER 28, THE GIFT

If I reflect Jesus with words that I write,
I'm not focused on "could have beens", shadows now past,
Or even the "shoulds", but instead on His light.
I'm focused on truths that are real and will last.

I prefer to point out that He offers us rest.
He shares all our burdens and carries the load.
He offers a way to know life at its best,
As we walk through each day toward the end of this road.

His love's beyond measure. He's gentle of heart.
He gave up His life so we truly can live.
His love's everlasting, will never depart.
There's no greater gift our Creator could give.

I pray that you've opened your gift and found love,
The greatest of gifts sent from heaven above.

NOVEMBER 29, TRANSFORMATION

As we open the Bible this time of the year
We tend to be focused on Luke chapter two,
The shepherds, the angels, the time they appear,
The babe in a manger, the animals too.

But I also remember what He left behind
To be born as the Christ child, to live here on earth.
He came down from glory to join humankind.
What a great transformation when Mary gave birth.

The master creator took on a new form.
There's no greater gift than the love that He gave.
He lay in a manger in rags to keep warm.
Then he gave us new life as He rose from the grave.

He's now back in glory. He sits on His throne,
The One who transforms us and calls us His own.

NOVEMBER 30, LISTENING

I'm not the most humorous, witty old chap.
I'm not full of great stories to make others laugh.
I'm not likely to speak just to fill in a gap,
Between listening and talking it's not half and half.

I love to hear stories that other folks tell,
Especially old folks who've lived a full life,
A look back at history they know it so well.
They remember the good times and also the strife.

We all have our stories, the good and the bad,
A stockpile of mem'ries we're building each day.
I pray there's some laughter to mix with the sad,
The sunshine that follows when rain comes our way.

Take time to listen, to make a new friend.
It's good for the soul. It will help a heart mend.

DECEMBER 1, A HUMBLE BIRTH

I'm not sure what traditions at Christmas you hold,
Or if you have any at all you observe,
But I pray you know Jesus, whom prophets foretold,
Who gave us a gift we've not earned nor deserve.

Born in a manger, no room in the inn.
His mother, a virgin, a carpenter's wife,
Gave birth to a Savior to die for our sins,
His mission, not easy, He gave up His life.

He gave up the glory of heaven above.
Grew up as a carpenter not as a king.
He spoke of His Father with mercy and love.
Now centuries later with songs we still sing

Of the humble surroundings the night He was born,
Just straw for His head, not a crown to adorn.

DECEMBER 2, ROOTS

I cherish my heritage, east Texas roots,
The mem'ries of Christmas, a new pair of boots,
The lights, decorations, the carols we sang,
I love country carols, a slight touch of twang.

Our house had some lights and a wreath with a bow,
Though cold in the winter we seldom saw snow.
I recall country churches, with benches for pews,
When times seemed so simple, we seldom had news.

Our tree was a cedar from granny's old place.
In my heart all the memories still have a space.
Our stockings were white and my daddy's size ten.
Santa stuffed them with fruit, nuts and candy back then.

I love all the mem'ries of Christmas each year.
They'll always be special, and cherished, and dear.

DECEMBER 3, CHRISTMAS PRAYER

I pray that this Christmas you're healthy and well.
If not, then I pray you're soon back on your feet.
I pray you have laughter and stories to tell.
I pray you have shelter and plenty to eat.

I pray you know peace, find some time to reflect
On the ways you've been blessed on your journey to here.
Taking time to be grateful we sometimes neglect.
Identify milestones and blessings each year.

I pray if you're faced with a major life change
That you find all the courage you need to endure,
And the strength to adapt, to adjust, rearrange.
I pray that your faith remains steady and sure.

I pray most of all you have love in your heart
From the One who was born with God's gift to impart.

DECEMBER 4, SIMPLE WORDS

I love to write rhyme it's just something I do.
My writing's straight forward not hard to construe.
My poems are quite simple, no need to explain.
They're easy to read, some would say they are plain.

If I look to my heart for my words, not my head.
Perhaps they'll touch others, be shared, and be read.
I pray they help others to reach deep inside,
Make room in their heart, let God's Spirit reside.

God sent His Son Jesus to die in our place.
He lay down His life for the whole human race.
Yet so many still mock Him rejecting His love,
His gift of salvation sent down from above.

May my words spread the news there is joy to be found.
As we celebrate Christmas may His love abound.

DECEMBER 5, OLD SONNETS

We respect the old poets, each line that they wrote,
Like musical lyrics in need of a note.
We love the old verses, the crafting, the style,
They lodge in the heart and they stay for a while.

We quote the old sonnets, the stories they tell.
They roll off the lips and they linger so well.
My rhyme and my rhythm may be out of date,
Perhaps I'm old fashioned or born a bit late.

I waited quite late and I'm well past my prime,
But this is the season when I had the time,
Discovered my passion, now writing each day.
It gives me great pleasure, it's my form of play.

If I choose the right words as I pen each refrain,
Perhaps a few lines of my rhymes will remain.

DECEMBER 6, TWILIGHT TRANSFORMATION

In the twilight of years that I have that remain
The Lord's blessed me with words that take root in my heart
Then transform into rhythm and rhyme in my brain.
I pray as I write them His love I impart.

It is hard to explain how this happened to me.
It's been quite a journey to find what's inside,
A mixture of feelings turned loose and set free.
The door to my soul I've now opened quite wide.

I have no regrets about words I have shared.
Giving others a look, somewhat scary at first,
I doubted if anyone else really cared,
But perhaps there's a longing, a hunger, a thirst.

The Lord gave me peace and I overcame fear.
I pray they take root and bear fruit through the years.

DECEMBER 7, QUIET AND STILL

In the midst of the hustle of Christmas this year
I urge you to pause and to listen and hear.
Take time to be silent, just quiet and still.
Reflect on the prophets, their words were fulfilled.

The Christ Child was born as the prophets foretold.
His birth is remembered though centuries old.
It began in a manger where Mary gave birth.
God's Son became man and he lived on the earth.

Such humble beginnings for one to be king,
Predicted by prophets, of whom angels sing.
He came not to reign but to give and to serve,
To give us new life we've not earned nor deserve.

Take time to reflect, to give thanks and believe
The true gift of Christmas is yours to receive.

DECEMBER 8, THIS CHRISTMAS

Each Christmas is different with each passing year.
A day that is special gets marked in our mind,
Fond mem'ries of loved ones, those no longer here.
We're still making mem'ries we too leave behind.

Find time for the dear ones who need it the most.
Cherish the moments, they soon will be past.
It's more than the gifts and the parties we host.
It's love, not the present, that truly will last.

The friendships, the memories etched in my soul
Make every year special and different somehow.
I pray that this Christmas, whatever unfolds,
I'll cherish the moments, the here and the now.

I pray that this Christmas brings joy to your heart.
God's love's everlasting, will never depart.

DECEMBER 9, CHRISTMAS NOSTALGIA

I tend toward nostalgic this time of the year.
Past Christmases whisper inside of my ear.
Reminders to cherish the ones that remain.
It's more about giving, it's not about gain.

A time to reach out to each other in love,
Recall how the angels sang praises above,
Gave glory to God, proclaimed peace on the earth
The night in a manger that Mary gave birth.

It's a time to remember, to be of good cheer.
May the joy of the season be with us all year.
May the love in our hearts find a way to be shared.
May our words and our actions show others we care.

Remember the Christ child who taught s to give.
He gave up His life so that others may live.

DECEMBER 10, THE ANGEL SPOKE

Inside my heart in song I sing,
Rejoice God sent His Son to earth,
To reign on high, a newborn King.
The angel came, announced His birth.

The shepherds watching o'er their herd,
Upon a hill that starry night,
The angel spoke, his voice they heard.
They saw God's glory shining bright.

A host of angels joined in song.
Sang praises to the Lord on high
In harmony the heavenly throng
With melody that filled the sky.

The shepherds went to Bethlehem,
Found Mary, Joseph, and the child.
They shared the angel's words with them,
A special moment, tender, mild.

A baby's birth, so long foretold.
For centuries it's been retold.

DECEMBER 11, A CHRISTMAS CAROL

A Christmas Carol features Scrooge,
His load of greed was old and huge,
Forgotten love replaced by gold,
His crusty heart, no warmth, just cold.

We all have ghosts of Christmas past,
Some shattered dreams dark shadows cast,
Impacting still our lives today.
We still can choose a brighter day.

The Christmas future's in our heart,
We have a choice, a brand-new start.
Reach out to those you love and know,
And let them see your love, your glow.

Find ways to show your love and care,
Let love and kindness fill the air.

DECEMBER 12, JOY OF THE SEASON

May the joy of the season, the still of the night
Bring peace on the earth until dawn's early light.
May the Light end the darkness, our sight to restore.
Embrace what is good and love others once more.

With so many so needy, so many in pain,
Take time to share love, we have so much to gain.
Let hate be defeated, let's give love a chance,
Break forth in laughter, in song, and in dance.

It's easy to say but much harder to do,
Letting go of the past and embracing the new.
Refocus on others find ways to reach out.
Love that is shared is what life's all about.

God sent us His love, let it fill every space.
I pray in your heart you've prepared Him a place.

DECEMBER 13, LOVE LINGERS

It's already December and Christmas draws near.
It's a time of reflection, reviewing this year.
I pray that the joyful days outweighed the sad.
I pray that the new year approaching brings glad.

It's a time to remember the Christmases past,
Those mem'ries we cherish that linger and last.
So many good people, the ones we have loved,
Have gone on to glory in heaven above.

The love that they left is still with us today,
Their love still remains and will linger and stay.
Love never runs out, always more we can give.
I pray I share love every day that I live.

May the message of Christmas be spread through the earth.
Love took human form the night Mary gave birth.

DECEMBER 14, REFLECTIONS

The season, the carols, nostalgia and lore
Built up through the Christmases decades and more,
Those images, memories, swim in my head,
The stories I've lived and the ones I have read.

It's easy to let expectations take hold,
Decorations and lights and the stories of old.
It's not about tinsel or fashion or trends,
The time I love most is with family and friends.

The love and the friendship we find here on earth,
Reflections of glory, a virgin gave birth.
We celebrate Christmas, the birth of a child,
Born in a manger, so meek and so mild.

May we be a reflection at Christmas this year,
As we reach out to friends, to the ones we hold dear,
May the meaning of Christmas abide in our heart,
Stay with us this Christmas and never depart.

DECEMBER 15, CELEBRATE JESUS

The sights and the sounds of the season are here,
Advertisements reminding us Christmas is near.
The songs usher memories cherished and dear.
As a child I learned stories of one silent night.

He was born in a manger, a trough for a bed,
A bundle of straw as support for His head,
In a place where the animals normally fed,
While a star in the sky guided kings with its light.

An angel told shepherds, "Good tidings I bring."
They heard thousands of angels in harmony sing.
They were led to the stable to honor the King,
Beheld baby Jesus, a glorious sight.

May this Christmas build memories joyful and bright,
As we celebrate Jesus our source of delight.

DECEMBER 16, SHELTER ME

When days grow weary, full of care
Reach out to God, He's always there.
The Lord can ease the deepest pain.
Find rest in Him, our cares will wane.

He calms our fears, and brings us peace,
Restores our hope, all worries cease.
In Him we trust to make a way.
He gives us strength we need each day.

Though storms may rage, be still, be blessed.
Wrapped in His arms find perfect rest.
In cold dark days inside the storm,
You shelter me and keep me warm.

When weary Lord, I trust in You.
I know You care. You get me through.
You lift me up and help me see
Your everlasting love for me.

DECEMBER 17, THE SHEPHERDS

I didn't hear the angels sing,
Or see the star that led three kings,
But on that night so long ago,
The shepherds saw the sky aglow.

On that extraordinary night
Those chosen shepherds saw the light.
They gathered 'round, beheld the Son.
They worshipped Him, the Holy One.

Selected they would be the first,
Bear witness to the holy birth.
The manger scene with shepherds, sheep,
Traditions to this day we keep.

The shepherds help us all to see
God sent His Son for you and me.

DECEMBER 18, THE ANGELS

The angels delivered their message that night,
Magnificent creatures, wings glowing and bright.
The heavens rang out with their glorious song
A baby is born to make right all the wrong.

Those glorious creatures a sight to behold,
Their message that night would forever be told,
Proclaimed with a trumpet, the sound of a horn,
Would be sung through the ages, "A Savior is born."

Those choirs of angels in heaven still sing
Proclaiming His majesty, Jesus our King.
No room in the inn, they had no place to stay,
Born in a manger, His head on the hay.

He came not with robes, nor with riches or gold,
He came as a Savior as prophets foretold.
He came down in love as a gift to mankind,
He gave us His life, there's none greater we'll find.

DECEMBER 19, FIGHT LONELINESS

When Christmas comes around this year,
Whose voice is it you long to hear?
A parent, brother, sister, spouse,
No longer here, they're in God's house.

Fight loneliness, push back the gloom,
May friends and love light up your room.
May memories of Christmas past
Embrace your heart, love's shadow cast.

Don't let the present slip away.
Find ways to show your love today,
A simple smile, a word or deed,
Reach out to touch someone in need.

Each day from God's a precious gift.
Help other souls who need a lift.

DECEMBER 20, GOD'S SON

The children long for Christmas Day
And wish that it could always stay.
The Christmas spirit need not leave.
Reach out in love and trust, believe.

It's not about the lights, the bows.
God's Son brought life when He arose.
His love brings joy inside our hearts,
A lasting peace that won't depart.

The shepherds heard the angels sing.
God sent His Son, a newborn King.
We celebrate that holy night.
He is the everlasting light.

The greatest story ever told,
Reach out in faith let love take hold.

DECEMBER 21, CHRISTMAS MEMORIES

Aromas of cinnamon cider with clove
Emerge from the kettle kept hot on the stove.
The holly and mistletoe, bells on the door,
Stuffed bears and the carolers stand on the floor.

The sights and the smells that bring Christmas to mind,
Those memories linger so fragrant, so kind.
Each year those traditions and visions return,
Residing within me, still there to discern.

Though I find myself grayer and life's a bit slow,
I still enjoy Christmas with candles that glow.
The manger displayed on the mantle with love,
Reminders that Jesus came down from above.

I pray that your memories bring you great joy,
Like those that I started as just a small boy.

DECEMBER 22, SHARED MEMORIES

I'm always surprised I keep writing each day,
Mostly surprised I have something to say.
I'm not really shy, just not gifted with gab.
I'm more prone to listen, less likely to blab.

I guess I find writing more easily shared.
I can tinker with words forming lines that will pair.
I'm less likely to write what I'll later regret
With a chance to review, and revise 'til they're set.

With old friends there's no need for a backspace, erase.
There's nothing like friendship, a hug or embrace,
Swapping stories, remembering times from the past,
How even today we see shadows they cast.

Though not often together old friendships endure.
Hold onto the mem'ries and keep them secure.

DECEMBER 23, CHRISTMAS EVE GIFT

Another Christmas Eve is near.
It's more than lights and mistletoe.
Take time to pause, reflect this year.
Reach out in love to those you know.

Perhaps someone who needs a lift
Could use some simple words of hope.
Perhaps your time's the perfect gift,
Encouragement to help them cope.

I pray the words I pen in rhyme
Encourage you, show love and care.
Should they withstand the test of time,
Perhaps live on as others share,

I pray that others find God's love,
Embrace His gift sent from above.

DECEMBER 24, CHRISTMAS EVE

It's Christmas Eve another year,
Another Christmas almost here.
I don't know what the year will bring,
What kind of song my heart will sing.

We stand four generations tall.
The first great grand she came last fall.
One more to come, two months away.
Now we're the ones adorned with grey.

The Christmases go by so fast,
Build memories, the love will last.
Traditions fade but new ones form,
Some old, some new, become the norm.

No matter how traditions change,
How we adapt and rearrange,
We celebrate the Savior's birth,
The day He came to dwell on earth.

DECEMBER 25, CHRISTMAS MORNING

Good Christmas morning everyone.
That long awaited day is here.
We celebrate God sent His Son.
Give thanks we've made another year.

As children gather 'round the tree,
To see if Santa brought a toy,
Take time to pray, to bend a knee,
Within your heart find peace and joy.

Perhaps the kids by now are grown,
They've all moved on to find their way.
God came to earth, you're not alone.
That's why we celebrate this day.

God's gift was wrapped in rags for clothes
Sent down for you, he saw your worth.
His gift's for you, the one He chose.
Accept His gift, a second birth.

DECEMBER 26, BEYOND CHRISTMAS

Take the wreath down from the door,
No longer Christmas anymore.
Another year's about to start.
I pray the love stays in our heart.

I pray good will is here to stay,
That angry hate will fade away.
God sent His Son to set us free.
May eyes once blind begin to see.

No matter what the year may bring,
I pray our hearts once more may sing.
His love extends through time and space.
I pray God's people seek His face.

Get on our knees before we stand,
And pray for peace throughout the land.

DECEMBER 27, CHRISTMAS LINGERS

From many scenes of Christmas past,
Some linger still, their shadows cast.
The warmth, the love they still endure
Like gold, refined that's clean and pure.

A smile, a touch, a warm embrace,
The sparkle of a baby's face
All linger in my heart and mind,
The memories, the ties that bind.

Some memories in lost and found
Come back when triggered by a sound.
A melody, a song or phrase
Stir memories obscured by haze.

Those cherished memories I hold
Still warm my heart when nights grow cold.

DECEMBER 28, WORDS AND THOUGHTS

My thoughts once remained in obscurity
Until I decided that they should be free.
I opened the cage and they learned how to fly,
To glide on their wings as they soar through the sky.

They love to take flight, to look down from above,
Find peace and tranquility, freedom they love.
Some things that they see as they search and explore
Can only be seen from the heights as they soar.

They show me new places that I might have missed,
New words and new vistas to add to my list.
Sometimes I'm surprised what direction they lead,
The places they take me those thoughts that I've freed.

Once they're set free and no longer inside,
The words can reach others there's no need to hide.

DECEMBER 29, LIFE UNCERTAIN

Life is uncertain not always the same.
It's constantly changing and hard to explain.
It's fruitless to dwell on how things might have been,
To dwell on what's happened, the past way back then.

The present and future we mold, we can shape,
But changes will come that we cannot escape.
Surrounded by changes some small, others vast,
The present is fleeting, a blink and it's past.

An anchor to steady our boat in the storm,
To keep us afloat when the waves threaten harm,
Brings peace in the midst of the winds in a gale.
In the calm of the morning, we'll once again sail.

God's Son is the anchor to keep us afloat.
He's willing and able to steady our boat.

DECEMBER 30, REMINISCING

As I look back across a full year in review,
I've left in my path some debris still askew.
So much in my life that is due for a change,
To fix or to mend or at least rearrange.

Some years seem more difficult, hard to survive,
Little time left to focus on what makes me thrive.
When I turn inward, neglect others' needs,
It's easy to stray off the trail in the weeds.

I want to reach out and to find ways to share,
To offer assistance to those who need care,
But I don't always know how to help with their pain,
To help them recover, their strength to regain.

I pray as I write that the words that I rhyme
Will offer encouragement, help in due time.
I pray as I share of my journey through life,
That I can help others find peace amidst strife.

The journey's not over, so much left to write,
I pray that I'm able to share love and light.

DECEMBER 31, ENDURE

The trees now bare they've shed their leaves
The winter's come to usher cold
For some the time has come to grieve
Enduring pain as life unfolds

A time to mourn, to shed a tear
I pray for those who now feel lost
I pray that peace replace the fear
Find memories well worth the cost

I pray that time will ease the pain
Once more renew the will to live
That joy once more the heart regain
Find ways to love, to serve, to give

Beyond the winter comes the spring
Endure for now, once more you'll sing

ABOUT THE AUTHOR

John writes books that appeal to elementary school children to capture their imagination and help them discover the love of reading early in life as well as inspirational poetry books. John lives in Frisco, Texas with his beautiful wife and his Cavalier King Charles Spaniel.

John spent his childhood in a small town in east Texas. He attended college at the University of Texas earning degrees in Physics and Math, then spent many years developing innovative communications systems. While still working, he began writing fiction in his spare time and published *The Enclave*, a mystery/suspense novel, in 2010.

Since leaving high tech in 2014, he now spends full time pursuing his writing passion. He especially loves writing books that help elementary school children discover that reading is a fun adventure. The chapter books in the Amber-Autumn mystery series, including *Christmas Garden*, *Grandfather's Blessing*, *Golden Campout*, and *The Secret Room* appeal to elementary school children.

John discovered his love for rhyme and released his debut book of poetry, *Timeless Tales*, in 2018. His first picture book, *Words That Soar*, won first place at the 2019 North Texas Book Festival. *The Christmas Gift*, published by Elk Lake Publishing, Inc, came out in 2019. His debut unpicture book, The Young Artist, came out in 2020. Two other picture books, *The Velveteen Rabbit Lyrical Rendition* and *Donkey Tale* followed in 2022 and 2023. His poetry books, *Quiet Tine Rhymes: Peace in the Pandemic*, released 2020, and *Quiet Time Rhymes Volume II: Into the Light* released 2021. His first book of daily poems, *Daily Reflections: 365 Lyrical Poems* released in 2021. This book continues with volume II. Other poetry collections include *Celebrate Christmas* and *In Times of Grief.*

www.ingramcontent.com/pod-product-compliance
Lightning Source LLC
Chambersburg PA
CBHW060237100426
42742CB00011B/1555